IMPLEMENTING CROSS-CURRICULAR THEMES

Keith Morrison

David Fulton Publishers Ltd
2 Barbon Close, London WC1N 3JX

First published in Great Britain by
David Fulton Publishers 1994

Note: The right of Keith Morrison to be identified as the author of this work has been asserted by him in accordance with the Copyright, Designs and Patents Act 1988.

Copyright © Keith Morrison

British Library Cataloguing in Publication Data

A catalogue record for this book is available from the British Library

ISBN 1-85346-313-2

Typeset by Action Ty tting Lim   lo ester
Printed in Great   Melksham

Contents

Acknowledgements

E. English, Headteacher, Ouston Infant School, Co. Durham, for material for figures 3.15 and 3.18; S. Inman for questions and lists of concepts from pp. 18–34 of *Curriculum Guidance No. 1 – Whole School Provision for Personal and Social Development: The Role of the Cross Curricular Elements,* the first of two Curriculum Guidance documents from the Centre for Cross Curricular Initiatives (an INSET, consultancy, publications and research centre), Goldsmiths' College, University of London; B. Lowes, Headteacher, Ouston Junior School, Co. Durham, for material for figures 3.15, 3.17 and 3.18; Sr. A. Ryan, Headteacher, Esh Laude RC School, Co. Durham, for material for figure 3.16.

Preface

A school is not merely a teaching shop; it transmits values and attitudes (CACE, 1967). It is a place where students come to find out about the world and about themselves in that world. Effective teaching should build on the intense interest that students show in the world around them. Indeed, developing the individual is a necessary part of developing society.

Change in education is occurring at an exponential rate; it is difficult to predict what knowledge, skills and understandings the present generation of students will be using in ten years' time and what they will need by the time they are in mid-career. More than at any time before students need to understand the societies and cultures of which they are members. Citizens of the twenty-first century will have to be able to assimilate the information revolution and to accommodate themselves to it. That requires the exercise of active and informed choice and the ability to be adaptable to changing circumstances. For their part schools will have to cultivate students' abilities to understand society and develop their abilities to be active participants in it.

The cross-curricular themes of the national curriculum of England and Wales have a major and exciting contribution to make in this respect. With the slimming down of the national curriculum advocated by the Dearing Commission (SCAA, 1993a) and more discretion given to schools to decide the content of the whole curriculum diet for children, there is an opportunity for more time to be given to this important aspect of the curriculum. There can be no doubt that the cross-curricular themes of the national curriculum constitute one of the most important innovations in school curricula. No aspect of the curriculum is left untouched by them. There is a pressing need for the significance of their message to be translated into everyday school practice. This book maps out a way of meeting this need. In this process a significant focus is placed on five of the *Curriculum Guidance* documents from the former National Curriculum Council. These are short but seminal texts which schools can use in building curricula. The cross-curricular themes present a marvellous opportunity for new and innovating curricula to be built, for schools to develop collegiality, and for students actively to appropriate their own learning. It is an opportunity which should be seized with both hands.

The book provides guidance on how this opportunity can be realized. It takes the reader through a series of building blocks of the curriculum (eg aims, objectives, planning strategies, delivery, organization, pedagogy and assessment) and suggests how these can be interpreted with reference to the five cross-curricular themes. More that this, the book regards the introduction of the themes as a major innovation. It sets out the implications of this and indicates how the themes can be developed in school. It regards the planning and implementation of the cross-curricular themes as an important means of developing teamwork and leadership in school. In turn these foster a healthy school climate which is conducive to effective teaching and learning.

Each chapter sets out a range of relevant issues in planning the implementation of the cross-curricular themes and generates criteria for evaluating the cross-curricular themes and their impact on students. These are brought together in the final chapter on evaluation. With the rise of school *inspections* and *school development plans* the spotlight has been turned onto the *processes* of education. This book specifically addresses these issues and indicates how the planning of the cross-curricular themes can meet the requirements of inspections and school development planning.

The book begins with aims and objectives, then, in sequence, moves through chapters on planning (content), pedagogy, assessment, change and innovation to evaluation. One can see in this overall organization more that a spectre of elements of curriculum planning which have been developed from Tyler (1949), through Skilbeck (1984) to the contemporary debate on the role of critical theory in curriculum building (Morrison, 1989). However, disembodied 'theory' is not allowed to surface more than is absolutely necessary as the intention here is to provide a series of *practical* considerations which are rooted in sound educational theory. Hence relevant theory often is given in references and in end notes to each chapter.

Education is about people; this book treats the planning and implementation of this major innovation as concerning people as much as curriculum content. Education is not simply a process of receiving meanings and curricula; it is about creating meanings and enabling students to create meanings. This book argues that the cross-curricular themes of the national curriculum present a window of opportunity to develop creativity, autonomy and social responsiblity in students. This will occur as the issues that they treat are interrogated and problematised; it is an opportunity within the grasp of teachers and students. The message of the book is that the development of the cross-curricular themes empowers all the participants in the educational process – teachers, students and the community beyond school. This book strives to be part of that process of empowerment.

Keith Morrison
University of Durham

CHAPTER ONE

The Aims of the Cross-Curricular Themes

The philosophers have only *interpreted* the world, in various ways; the point, however, is to change it. (Marx)

Society has devolved upon schools in large part the responsibility to prepare its future citizens to cope with change – the abilities to stand upright when all around is changing. There is a need for students to be adaptable and flexible as never before. The school has a task to prepare students for life outside and beyond school.

In an era which is characterised by change the need for personal and social education is more pressing than ever. If students are to understand a changing society and are to become active members of it, then a passive, academic education has to be complemented by an active, enquiring education which is grounded in the issues of everyday life. Education should empower students and societies to shape their own and collective futures. Empowerment – the ability of individuals and groups to realise and enrich their own futures in a free and egalitarian society – sets its own agenda. This comprises a questioning of values, legitimacy and the politics of decision-making. It examines equality, privilege, advantage and disadvantage. The school curriculum is inescapably political. This is its excitement and its frustration! Decisions on its content are not arbitrary; they represent values, purposes and interests. Education is the process of rendering these transparent.

In this process it is not enough that students should possess a body of knowledge. They also need to know what to do with it and how it enables them to be active participants in society. Indeed a lesser known line from Marx's *Theses on Feuerbach* than that which prefaced this chapter begins: 'Social life is essentially *practical*'.

The content and pedagogy of the cross-curricular themes, as part of every child's entitlement to the national curriculum of England and

Wales, constitute a major means by which individual and collective empowerment can be realised, as they concern raising students' awareness of major contemporary issues. The importance of the cross-curricular themes in the school curriculum cannot be overstated. In some part this is recognized by the publication of the eight *Curriculum Guidance* documents by the National Curriculum Council in 1989 and 1990. This chapter outlines the strengths and weaknesses of the five *Curriculum Guidance* documents which set out the cross-curricular themes and indicates how the cross-curricular themes can serve individual and social empowerment.

The national curriculum meets change by providing a centrally prescribed, subject-based, uniform curriculum which is academic in character and which is legitimated by the force of statute. In this curriculum one can see that some types of knowledge are elevated to a higher status than others. At the top of the ladder come the core subjects of the national curriculum; next come the foundation subjects. At the bottom of the ladder come the cross-curricular themes, lacking the force of law to ensure that they find a place in the school curriculum. A subject-based, academic, curriculum which relies on the written word and is formally assessed does little to upset the societal *status quo*[1]. It is 'socially reproductive' rather than 'socially transformative'.

Even though there is formal equality of opportunity of access to an entitlement curriculum, writers from Bourdieu (1976) to Halsey (1992) demonstrate that providing equality of access to an academic curriculum is insufficient to produce equality of outcomes for students. By dint of their different class, gender, racial backgrounds and possession of 'cultural capital' students will take up an academic curriculum differentially. Those for whom school knowledge is an extension of the knowledge that they receive at home are advantaged over students for whom school knowledge represents an alien culture. One can question the motives of a government which elevates the socially *reproductive* elements of the national curriculum and lowers the status of its socially *transformative* elements.[2] Those areas which will challenge the societal *status quo* are accorded low status, those that will not, receive high status. Indeed, as if to avert challenge to the *status quo,* some contentious social issues are not mentioned in the national curriculum, for example media studies, peace education, women's studies.

It is in the low-status cross-curricular themes that the potential to meet the demands of a changing society find their clearest expression. This can be evidenced in several ways. The content of the cross-curricular themes trades in 'dangerous knowledge' (Giroux, 1983), ie that knowledge which can challenge traditional values and assumptions. They are inextricably and unavoidably linked to the values and practices in the wider society. They have external referents which cannot be bounded within the school, as they explore community links. They examine political decision-making and infrastructures of society. Their subject matter is not confined to academicism but to politics and its ramifications in the society beyond school Their subject matter deals with sensitive issues – the politics of ecological and environmental decision-making and health care, employment and membership of a capitalist society, being a citizen of several communities. Go through the Curriculum Guidance documents for the cross-curricular themes and you will find that it is in these that the seeds of social change and an examination of the social fabric of everyday life are sown. Their impact can be unsettling and uncomfortable. Little wonder it is, perhaps, that they are relegated to a non-statutory, non-examined, low status area of the school curriculum by a government with a history of interventionist policies on the curriculum. Since the Education Reform Act of 1988 (DES, 1988a) the government in office has exerted considerable control of the objectives, content and assessment of the curriculum. Clearly the notion of a broad entitlement curriculum which every state school has a duty to provide might be more empowering that its predecessors. The question, however, is whether this is sufficient to guarantee full student empowerment in a changing world.

The national curriculum redefines student empowerment as the achievement of somebody else's prescriptions. The curriculum is a 'given', its purposes, values and goals are not susceptible to debate, the teacher simply decides how best to teach it. The only area where prescription gives way to suggestion is in the cross-curricular themes by dint of their non-statutory status. It is in these that greater freedoms can occur.

However, let me not be merely negative about the national curriculum for it is concerned to foster *understanding* of curriculum content. It is not simply rote learning in the tradition of Gradgrind. The documents of the national curriculum are replete with terms such as 'understand', 'identify', 'know that', 'describe' etc.

However there remains a requirement that students will still receive a prespecified curriculum. The national curriculum signally understates the need for *critique* and *interrogation* of issues and of the *legitimacy* of values; indeed it regards as unquestionable its prescriptions for curricular knowledge. The *agenda* of the national curriculum remains unaltered.[3]

If we want to develop students' adaptability and their ability to

4

behave proactively in a changing world then simply receiving and understanding curricula has to be complemented by a critique of curricula and the issues and values implicit in them. A concern with empowerment – individual and collective – will require a critique of ideology and of whose and what interests are being served by curricula. The message here is the one from Marx which headed this chapter. Understanding has to be accompanied by critique in a climate of change.[4]

The contents of the cross-curricular themes are a potent means for the development of empowerment, for the topics that they cover contain knowledge that has the potential to challenge the *status quo* (outlined earlier). If teachers and students are to do justice to the politically and ideologically problematical areas of the cross-curricular themes it is unavoidable that they will have to engage questions of legitimacy. They will have to expose and debate the interests of those possessed of power – political, economic, gender-related etc. – as they are introduced in the cross-curricular themes.

Whilst the cross-curricular themes have potential for empowerment it is necessary to devote specific additional attention to issues of legitimacy, ideology critique, politics, power and decision-making if this potential is to be realized. Curriculum planners can turn to their own advantage the *non-statutory* nature of the cross-curricular themes by introducing these sensitive issues into the curriculum.

It is not only in decisions about curriculum *content* that empowerment lies. One could have a curriculum whose content was politically and ideologically explosive yet whose explosive potential was never realized in practice. Students could study 'dangerous' knowledge in a way which defuses critique and empowerment by engaging in understanding rather than critical exploration of issues. What is required is attention to *pedagogy,* for it is in human relationships, interactions and ways of addressing knowledge that the potential for empowerment in the cross-curricular themes can be released.

The *Curriculum Guidance* documents suggest that appropriate teaching and learning styles are premissed on active, experiential learning. They argue for links to the community outside the school to be made and that contacts with organizations and groups outside schools are necessary. Further, they suggest that collaborative, problem-solving approaches should be adopted. Whilst these are discussed more fully in chapter four they are mentioned here because they indicate that not only does the curriculum *content* of the cross-curricular themes address referents beyond the school but that the *pedagogy* also suggests the need for links to be drawn between the school and the community. Hence students will be involved in participatory forms of learning, learning about democracy and group membership by working democratically and in groups (cf Harwood, 1985).

Curriculum content and pedagogy will need to combine to interrogate the content of the cross-curricular themes in order to develop student empowerment. In particular the planning and implementation of the cross-curricular themes will have to enable students and teachers to expose and debate the values implicit in these themes as they are addressed in the *Curriculum Guidance* documents and to indicate how a less partial, partisan interpretation of the themes might be undertaken. This is the object of the remainder of this chapter, where each theme is examined for the values implicit in it. These are exposed, critically examined and then, for each theme, a further set of values is established which, it is suggested, enable empowerment to be developed. It is argued that for each document an alternative, more empowering interpretation can be developed. The discussion indicates how this can be realized.

A critique of the *Curriculum Guidance* documents

During 1989 and 1990 the NCC issued a series of eight Curriculum Guidance documents, principally to cover the cross-curriculum area of the national curriculum:

- *A Framework for the Primary Curriculum* (NCC, 1989a);
- *A Curriculum for All* (NCC, 1989b);
- *The Whole Curriculum* (NCC, 1990a);
- *Education for Economic and Industrial Understanding* (NCC, 1990b);
- *Health Education* (NCC, 1990c);
- *Careers Education and Guidance* (NCC, 1990d);
- *Environmental Education* (NCC, 1990e);
- *Education for Citizenship* (NCC, 1990f).

At first blush the five cross-curricular themes mentioned as the last five of these documents possess the empowering potential alluded to earlier for they concern life and decision making in a changing world. They concern knowledge of (a) the economic motors of society and their effects on the democratic process, (b) how political and economic decisions affect the quality of life – environmentally, personally and interpersonally, and (c) the powers which an understanding of citizenship can bring. However, as will be seen below, for a full realization of their empowering potential the cross-curricular themes will need to add critique to mere understanding. What follows is an analysis of the *Curriculum Guidance* documents which deliberately intends to show that, though they provide a valuable starting point for developing student empowerment in a changing world, a 'different story' can be told about each cross-curricular theme. A full and rounded experience of the cross-curricular themes will need to address not only the story as it appears in the *Curriculum Guidance* documents but alternative interpretations of issues delineated in them.[5]

Education for Economic and Industrial Understanding

There is a recognition by the NCC that this theme 'involves controversial issues such as government economic policy and the impact of economic activity on the environment' (NCC, 1990b, p. 4). However in the same paragraph the message is given unequivocally that young minds should be educated to enable pupils to be embryonic capitalists in a free market, materialist economy:

> Education for economic and industrial understanding aims to help pupils make decisions such as how to organise their finances and how to spend their money . . . It prepares pupils for their future roles as producers, consumers and citizens in a democracy. Pupils need to understand enterprise and wealth creation and develop entrepreneurial skills (ibid., p. 4).

Indeed the tone of the NCC carries all the optimism of a wealthy populace whose only contribution to the economy is through work:

> They will face choices about how they contribute to the economy through their work. They will decide how to organise their finances and which goods and services to spend money on. (NCC, 1990b, p.1).

This renders unproblematic the reality of unemployment amongst individuals and whole communities which the demands of capital – corporate and international – exact in their drive for surplus value. It links the notion of citizenship very firmly with the economy, as though one cannot be a true citizen if one is not producing or consuming products:

> It prepares them for future economic roles: as producers, consumers and citizens in a democracy (ibid., p. 1).

In doing so it links democracy with the economy, a potentially narrow view of the complexity of democracy (cf Apple, 1993a).

Further, whilst it acknowledges the need for an understanding of an industrialised and highly technological society this document regards as unchallengeable and legitimate the view that society is premised on competitiveness (ibid., p. 1). Indeed the document does not see competitiveness as in any way problematic and consequently advocates increasing it. Indeed one becomes better at playing the game; pupils 'meet this challenge' by understanding wealth creation and developing entrepreneurial skills (ibid., p. 1) rather than by challenging the legitimacy of the game itself.[3] It commits the naturalistic – and ideological – fallacy of trying to derive an *ought* from an *is* – the fact that one can observe something occurring in society does not justify it. One wonders if the hard-nosed, challenging, combative style of the NCC document is essentially consistent with equal opportunities or with more caring, compassionate, collaborative ethics.

The title of this document and the tone throughout is also met in the other *Curriculum Guidance* documents from the National Curriculum Council – they deal with *understanding* rather than *critique*. The effects of this are to delegitimize alternatives and to legitimize the *status quo*. Equal opportunities becomes redefined as equal opportunity to play the same game regardless of the desirability of the game or its rules:

> All pupils, regardless of culture, gender, or social background, should have equal access to a curriculum which promotes economic and industrial understanding (NCC, 1990b, p. 6).

No space is given to the consideration that not everyone might wish to – or be able to – play the same game. Economic and industrial understanding is seen as a passionless activity. It is not idle, perhaps, to note that art, dance and drama – those aspects of the curriculum which could redeem the dehumanizing of economic and industrial education – all have their part to play in the early Key Stages (eg ibid., pp. 14, 15, 23, 24). However these are either absent in the later Key Stages or are redefined so as to serve advertising, marketing and persuasion to buy (e.g. pp. 33 and 42), as though they cease to be intrinsically important activities as children become locked into industrial and economic understanding.[6]

Further, people are seen as resources to be 'managed' efficiently or to be manipulated as consumers. The NCC document is unequivocal on this:

> Industry involves the effective management of people and other resources, and industrial organisations have different ways of maximising efficiency, output and job satisfaction (ibid, p. 41);

> Consumer decisions are influenced by prices, value for money, quality, advertising and personal circumstances (eg wealth). (ibid., p. 42).

This ignores questions of aims, values and goals – one simply accepts them as given. The EIU document sets clear boundaries about what is relevant to economic and industrial understanding (business, commerce, finance and consumer affairs) (ibid., p. 3) and defines 'controversial issues' in this field as 'the impact of economic activity on the environment', thereby minimising other controversial issues: poverty, class oppression, exploitative relationships, unequal power, the daily experience of racism and gender differentiation, the casualties of capitalism. Even though the document calls for a 'balanced presentation of opposing views' and for pupils to be 'encouraged to explore values and beliefs, both their own and those of others' (ibid., p. 3) its silence on what those might be is a most eloquent denial of their importance. It sees the rewards of wealth accruing to those individuals and communities possessed of 'business enterprise' (ibid., p. 4); it assumes that industry and industrial relations are fixed – *'the* organization of industry and industrial relations' (ibid., p. 4) (italics mine). It leaves the consideration of alternative economic systems until pupils have reached Key Stage four (ibid., p. 40) – a very late stage (for children in their middle teenage), by which time many of them will have become saturated with the values of the existing economic system.

However, the document has a certain antinomial quality. On the one hand what can be observed in it is the reaching into the heart of schools and very young children significant elements of society – money, law, economics. Indeed 'enterprise' is defined in terms which feed into wealth generation:

> Education for enterprise means two things. First, it means developing the qualities needed to be an 'enterprising' person, such as the ability to tackle problems, take initiatives, persevere, be flexible, and work in teams. Secondly, and more specifically, it means taking part in small-scale and community enterprise projects designed to develop these qualities (ibid., p. 6).

On the other hand one would hesitate to say that children ought *not* to be introduced to these issues. The question is one of adequacy. The document needs to inject critique early on in the Key Stages, it needs to widen its view of profit and loss to include human terms and humanity, it needs to question legitimacy, interests and ideology. It needs to take far more seriously and in a more developed way its own call for 'rational argument' (ibid., p. 5), for considerations of 'respect for alternative economic viewpoints and a willingness to reflect critically on their [pupils'] own economic views and values' and 'human rights' (ibid., p. 5). It needs to counter the view that education does not simply –

instrumentally – provide an economically desirable service, but that it is the bearer of 'dangerous knowledge', of critique and of the restoration of humanity in an age of technology.

Not only does the *content* of EIU neglect critique but this is evidenced in *pedagogy* – that element identified earlier as being important in promoting empowerment. Though the document implies active, experiential learning (for example: 'It means taking part in small scale business and community enterprise' (NCC, 1990b, p. 4), the pedagogical principles neglect critique. Figure 1.1 presents the key verbs used to describe the pedagogical aims of EIU at different stages.

Figure 1.1 – Key Verbs in the EIU Document

Key Stage	Key Verbs
KS1	Discuss; talk about; survey; visit
KS2	Discuss; understand; investigate; explore; visit; interview; examine; describe
KS3	Discuss; understand; survey; investigate; visit; compare; role-play; analyse; know that; recognise; collect data
KS4	Discuss; understand; collect; know; prepare; use; debate; investigate; identify

These terms neglect the higher order cognitive skills and reflect an interest in *understanding* rather than an interest in critique, judgement and evaluation. Indeed the only reference to evaluation shows it to be an evaluation of the achievement of given objectives rather than of the objectives themselves: 'Pupils were encouraged to reflect on and evaluate their own work in relation to the objectives for each part of the project' (ibid., p. 38). The EIU document, then, has potential for empowerment, the realization of which depends on the treatment which is given to its prescribed content and beyond.

Health Education

The NCC document (NCC, 1990c) casts health education into nine components:

- substance use and misuse;
- sex education;

- family life education;
- safety;
- health-related exercise;
- food and nutrition;
- personal hygiene;
- environmental aspects of health education;
- psychological aspects of health education.

The question to be put here is not against the content with which it deals − it would be difficult to argue against the inclusion of the content specified − but rather the way in which the content is approached. This will address the inclusion or exclusion of content and the hidden curriculum of such decision making.

A reading of the list of topics within health education might indicate that a wide range of issues and areas is to be covered; indeed that is the case. However, the document addresses the topics in such a way as to cast health education as largely an *individual's* responsibility, where this responsibility is merely an *exercise of choice*. For example the document indicates that 'today, non-infectious diseases, fatal accidents and unhealthy patterns of behaviour are the key factors' (ibid., p. 2). This minimizes environmental causes and avoids discussion of health problems overseas in developing and third world countries. Although problematical issues are alluded to on pp. 5, 13, 15, 17 and 20 they are defined in the early Key Stages as being a matter almost of individuals' responsibility which is subject to their own preference:

> Know that within any environment there are people with different attitudes, values and beliefs and that these influence people's relationships with each other and with the environment (ibid., p. 15).

As with the document *Education for Economic and Industrial Understanding* it is only in Key Stage 4 that reference is made to the politics of health care:

> understand how legislation and political, social, economic and cultural decisions affect health, (ibid., p. 20).

Even here the responsibility for health, as in the previous Key Stages, is overwhelmingly seen to be personal or at best a community concern − 'the overlapping interests of individual, group and community health' (ibid., p. 3). There is a silence on the large scale political decision-making to improve health care and provision. Further, the solubility of health problems is seen to be an individual rather than a political issue:

The emphasis in most health education curricula is on encouraging individual responsibility, awareness and informed decision-making (ibid., p. 7).

Such a circumscription of concerns diverts attention away from structural poverty and its relatedness to health, eg that many citizens cannot afford to exercise choice in their life styles, and that this is as much a politico-economic problem as it is a health problem. Though this is touched upon at Key Stage 3 (pupils should 'recognise that there are some socio-economic factors which make cleanliness more difficult for some people' (p. 17) there is a naivety about a document which can assert that students should:

> Know that there is a wide variety of foods to choose from and that choice is based on needs and / or culture (ibid., p. 13).

That, plainly, is an option for only a fraction of the world's population. The NCC document adopts a nationalistic, insular view of health at home as it impinges on children. It massively overlooks the international politics of health. Its assumption of the low incidence of infectious diseases overlooks third world poverty and the politics of international capitalism and international socialism which allows this to continue.

Whilst health education is seen to involve more than physiological concerns – extending to 'psychological aspects of health education', this is portrayed as relatively unproblematical. Hence the NCC document simplistically states that 'those who are happy with their image are able to take increasing control of their lives, including decisions relating to healthy lifestyles' (ibid., p. 9), overlooking the reality that for many the control of their image is out of their reach.

The NCC document is almost completely silent on the politics of health, thereby leaving the politics unchallenged. This silencing reaches further, for not only is the family unit (and, if the drawings in the document carry hidden messages, the white, nuclear family) celebrated as having the central role as an institution (p. 4) but alternative, less institutional groupings receive no comment. The document reinforces (both through its text and its drawings) the heterosexism and homophobia of a government which tried to outlaw homosexuality and its manifestations; sexual relationships are only to be heterosexual and only to be fostered in the context of supporting family life (ibid., p. 4). The celebration of the family unit disregards the lived experiences of many people of the miseries of family life (or its breakdown) and the happinesses of alternative groupings, whilst the silence on non-heterosexual relationships devalues minority groups in society. Both examples serve to reinforce the *status quo* which oppresses the already oppressed. This does little to further the equal opportunities policy declared as a cross-curricular dimension (NCC, 1989b). The issue is intensely political; Worsley (1977) summarizes a wealth of research to support the view that nuclear families underpin a capitalist economic system because of their characteristics of independence, privacy, consumerism, the exploitation of women, the facility for primary social relationships. Worsley argues that in many respects the value of the family unit is functionally convenient for the requirements of capital.

In terms of pedagogy health education is seen to be more a matter of understanding than of critique. As with the previous document, the political sensitivity of the issues, where it is addressed, is given only scant attention and then only at the later Key Stages. There is an assumption that children should not exercise their critical faculties until they reach teenage, and that sensitive issues cannot be made accessible to children at Key Stages 1 or 2. This runs counter to evidence (eg by Dixon, 1977) that race and gender stereotypes are present in pre-school children; it also neglects primary school teachers' everyday experiences of racism in young children. The NCC health education document only introduces the question of labelling and stereotyping at Key Stage 3.

If student empowerment is sought, then, as with the discussion of the previous document, this will require an amplification of the pedagogical sphere of health education to move beyond *understanding* of controversial issues to ideology critique and critical interrogation from the early Key Stages onwards of the sensitive issues of the document. This will include an examination of the legitimacy of the views propounded in the document, and the politics of the issues involved. What characterizes the health education document is its silence on the problematical underpinnings of its views. It devotes most of its pages to a laying out of content to be delivered rather than probing beneath the content to unpack the arguments and values which are contained in it.

The document does mention active, experiential forms of learning:

> The participation of pupils is essential in order to encourage pupils to learn from others and to help them use appropriate language in ways that are understood by others . . . [M]uch of the teaching in health education will be based on the active involvement of pupils. Teaching methods particularly suited to this kind of approach include games, simulations, case studies, role plays, problem-solving exercises, questionnaires, surveys, open-ended questions and sentences and group work of various kinds (NCC, 1990c, p. 7).

However this remains underdeveloped in the document. Further, Figure 1.2 indicates that, as with the document on EIU, the key verbs of this document use the language of understanding and accepting rather than of critique.

Figure 1.2 – Key Verbs in the Health Education Document

Key Stage	Key Verbs
KS1	Explore; construct; talk about; know that; understand; acquire
KS2	Devise; draw; exemplify; consider; perform; know that; understand; acquire; recognise
KS3	Discuss; describe; share; assess; identify; recognise; be aware of; understand; know that
KS4	Discuss; clarify; devise; investigate; explore; understand; be aware of, know that; accept

There is very little to suggest that pedagogical issues are sensitive, problematical and value laden. The potential for critical enquiry is minimized. If the legitimacy of decision making about health related issues (eg poverty, affluence, exploitation, health care and nutrition, and the political and economic systems which undergirded the decisions) were questioned then the empowering potential of health education might be unleashed. What we are presented with here is another commission of the naturalistic fallacy where an understanding of what *is* replaces a critical discussion of what *ought* to be happening in health related enquiry.

Careers Education and Guidance

This document (NCC, 1990d) argues that children will profit from an early contact with careers education which includes:

- careers education:
- access to information;
- experience of work;
- access to individual guidance;
- recording achievement and planning for the future. (NCC, 1990d, p. 5).

In this context careers education and guidance aims to promote personal and social development and challenge 'stereotyped attitudes to education, training and career opportunities' (ibid., p. 2) through the study of five strands:

- self (knowing oneself better);
- roles (being aware of education, training and career opportunities);
- work and career (making choices about continuing education and training, and about career paths);
- transition (managing transitions to new roles and situations).

In this process the document suggests the concept of *partnership,* developed through liaison between education and a variety of organizations and interested parties (pp. 9 – 10). It sees a clear and close link between careers education, education for industrial and economic understanding and citizenship. Indeed the document advocates the 'application of industrial processes in the classroom' (p. 5).

In discussing these links and partnerships the effect of this document is to suggest not only infinite possibility but also that the education system will prepare for this infinite possibility from the year a child enters school and thereafter be able to serve all of a child's career needs and interests. This is the optimism of the blind. It neglects the lived experiences of individuals and communities where (a) structural unemployment is an everyday feature, (b) the 'local employment patterns' (p. 30) are non-existent or fragile and temporary, (c) poor pay and conditions combine to render the concepts of a career and work not only worthless or unrealistic but undesirable, unfulfilling and undignifying. There is a cosiness about the document which suggests that if one abides by the advice given in it – if one 'plays the game' – then employment is certain, that 'future work opportunities' (p. 42) are guaranteed. Indeed the language of the document is replete with references to 'opportunities', 'motivation', 'career choices' and 'systematic career programmes'. The message is unequivocal: understand and abide by the rules of the game, do not challenge the 'system' and prosperity will follow; the 'system' is there to help. We come to love Big Brother.

The examples of careers which the document portrays are of fulfilling roles (eg p. 24), of 'admired adults' as role models (p. 29) and of the possibilities of work both at home and overseas (p. 40). The document is marked by the theme of 'possibility', which is unrealistic in an employment context which is market-driven, zero-sum, in which selection and competition for jobs occurs and in which 'opportunity' is defined as the opportunity to take part in a system whose legitimacy remains unchallenged.

The effects of wording the document in the ways observed are twofold. *Firstly* it diverts attention away from the desirability of the 'system' for which children are being prepared from the time they enter school (p. 12). *Secondly* it minimizes the problematic areas of the world of work, redefining the problem of work as the failure of an individual to match up to the system's requirements rather than *vice versa*. As with the previous two documents the study of controversial issues is not met until the Key Stages 3 and 4. Where these do appear they are given low priority by swamping them with a multiplicity of system-affirming areas of study (pp. 27–43). In these sixteen pages of text in the document there are only some two dozen lines in all which mention contentious issues. Understanding replaces critique, empowerment only follows if one abides by, rather than challenges, the system. The effects of this document are to delegitimize alternatives to the capitalist system, to neglect the lived experiences of unemployment and to render education instrumental, servicing a system the consideration of whose worth is circumscribed. It is interesting in this context to note the conservative nature of the example of a career line which stops at marriage (p. 29).

In terms of pedagogy the declared purposes have all the rhetoric of participatory activity (cf ibid., p. 5). However Figure 1.3 indicates that the verbs used in describing the pedagogy, whilst indicating that

Figure 1.3 – Key Verbs in the Careers Education Document

Key Stage	Key Verbs
KS1	Describe; form impressions; examine; plan; acquire; use; notice; identify; recognise; talk about; investigate
KS2	Understand; explore; become aware of; classify; review; compare; respond to; devise; visit; discuss; identify; use; contrast; anticipate
KS3	Understand; make decisions; solve problems; strengthen knowledge of; explore; compare; review; participate in; identify; survey; prepare for; consider; visit; research
KS4	Understand; prepare for; use; talk about; role-play; simulate; consult; compile; review; examine; share; identify; explore

possibilities for critique (eg 'begin to challenge adult role stereotypes' (p. 15) and 'consider controversial issues' (p. 31), nevertheless use the language of *understanding* rather than of *critique*.

As with the previous two documents, this document nevertheless carries some potential for empowerment. If the system is not simply accepted and understood but critically interrogated, if questions of interests, legitimacy and power are addressed, then careers education and guidance may be empowering. As with the previous two documents, this document provides a necessary introductory platform for enquiry but it needs to go further; it needs to introduce critique. The language of 'possibility' and 'opportunity' to 'know thyself' (NCC, 1990d) in careers education and guidance needs to take seriously the structural constraints and contexts which affect those possibilities and opportunities.

Environmental Education

Much of this document is devoted to worked examples of environmental education about, for and through the physical environment (NCC, 1990e, p. 7). It squarely reflects the contentious nature of environmental education and recognizes that 'environmental education is the subject of considerable debate and that there is no clear consensus about many of the issues' (ibid., p. 1). The document requires pupils to study a range of sensitive issues which raise questions of interests, legitimacy and ideology, for example:

- the impact of human activities upon the environment;
- environmental issues such as the greenhouse effect, acid rain, air pollution;
- local, national and international legislative controls to protect and manage the environment; how policies and decisions are made about the environment;
- the environmental interdependence of individuals, groups, communities and nations;
- the conflicts which arise about environmental issues;
- the importance of effective action to protect and manage the environment, (NCC, 1990e, p. 4).

Indeed the document suggest that environmental education aims to 'encourage pupils to examine and interpret the environment from a variety of perspectives – physical, geographical, biological, sociological, economic, political, technological, historical, aesthetic, ethical and spiritual' (ibid., p. 3). It suggests the need for a respect for evidence and rational argument (p. 6) and encourages individuals, schools and communities to raise awareness of personal, participatory responsibility for the environment (pp. 1−6).

Whilst this document is perhaps laudable it nevertheless stops short of challenging the powers of groups, governments and decision makers to exploit the environment, or the moral resolution of conflicts about environmental decisions. For instance, in the example of emissions from British power stations affecting Scandinavia (pp. 30−31) the nearest that the document comes to suggesting censure of the practice is to mention the need for 'environmental interdependence' (p. 30). In the passing mention it gives to rainforest destruction it neglects to consider the possible causes of rainforest destruction − eg materialist consumerism in the developed world, the developed world exploiting the third world − and the legitimacy of the enterprise. The document, like that on *Education for Economic and Industrial Understanding* considered above, gives weight to people as producers and consumers (p. 1) and some of the examples it gives, for example p. 39 on cattle rearing for profit, illustrate a market mentality. Justifications are seen pragmatically (eg. pp. 29 and 34) rather than ethically and questions of differential powers in decision making are understated. Access to, or influence over, decision makers is not considered problematical.

Figure 1.4 − Key Verbs in the Environmental Education Document

Key Stages	Key Verbs
KS1	Look at; express views on; compare; explore
KS2	Express views; argue; retrieve; interpret; evaluate; identify; investigate; form reasoned opinions
KS3	Investigate; analyse; take responsibility for; argue; retrieve; interpret; evaluate; identify; form reasoned opinions
KS4	Draw up proposals; argue; retrieve; interpret; evaluate; identify; form reasoned opinions

In terms of pedagogy this document suggests that environmental education 'introduces pupils to political processes and encourages them to take on social responsibility' (ibid., p. 12). In the verbs it uses this document possesses many elements of empowerment though it stops short of critique (Figure 1.4). One can see evidence in these terms of higher order thinking though it is interesting to note the same verbs appearing at three different stages, indicating either a lack of progression or a consistency of focus.

Hence, as with the problematical areas of the previous documents, the problematic questions of environmental education are mentioned – indeed they are seen to lie at the heart of environmental education. However they are cast in the language of unrealistic possibility. The case studies presented are either of local small scale projects or are paper exercises in analysis of more global issues. If student participation in decision making for environmental responsibility is sought then the channels of that participation and its problematical areas need to receive greater attention. One has, perhaps, to question the degree to which environmental education as construed in the document has the potential to bring about empowerment. Nevertheless this document, probably more than most of the others considered here, centralizes the problematical areas of the topic under discussion.

Education for Citizenship

The rhetoric of this document (NCC, 1990f) celebrates participatory democracy, positive action, responsibilities, rights and rational entitlement (p. 1), all central features of student empowerment. As with the previous documents discussed above, one would not wish much of the material to be excluded. Rather the question, as before, is how the material is treated and whether the material goes far enough to empower pupils. This document sets out an agenda of issues for citizenship education whose effects may reinforce the *status quo* and rule out of the analysis any developed questioning of legitimacy, interests, powers or degrees of freedom. There are two main ways in which this occurs.

Firstly, the document, in its aims of citizenship education, minimises critique in favour of understanding and delimits participatory action:

> Schools must lay the foundations for positive, participative citizenship in two important ways:
> (i) by helping pupils to acquire and understand essential information.
> (ii) by providing them with opportunities and incentives to participate in all aspects of school life. (NCC, 1990f, p. 1).

Thus pupils are only required to understand certain prescribed information, not to challenge it. Moreover, there is an arrogance in the certainty of what is 'the essential information' which rules out alternative constructions of essential information. Active participation is confined to school life rather than moving outside of school, it is contained in an environment that can leave the outside world untouched.

Secondly, when one examines the content of the citizenship curriculum one finds that its scope embraces:

(i)   *the nature of community involvement* (p. 5), which, even though it includes economic and political communities, only emphasises roles and the operation of these, ie they are 'givens', not interrogated;

(ii) *roles and relationships in a pluralist society* (p. 6), which, even though they emphasise equality, justice, multiculturalism and multiethnicity, nevertheless neglect to detail the problematical areas of these considerations, ie they are generalized, exhortatory and administered through the operation of laws whose content and legitimacy are not questioned;

(iii) *duties, responsibilities and rights of being a citizen* (pp. 6–7), which include reference to equal opportunities, political rights and the protection of the rights of the weak and disadvantaged, and recognize the need for a balance to be struck between individual freedoms and social constraints but which neglect to question the legitimacy of structural inequality, poverty, oppression and exploitation;

(iv) *the family* (p. 7) which, even though it includes an examination of the strengths and difficulties of family life, neglects to render the family as problematical (see the comments earlier on the health education document). In its celebration of the family and silence on other forms of partnerships it operates a heterosexism which violates the NCC's declared policy of equal opportunities and legitimates what, for many, is a problematical and illegitimate institution;

(v)   *democracy in action* (pp. 7–8) which, even though it includes a comparison of different political systems, is silent on the legitimacy or questioning of political systems and mechanisms of the state. The effects of this are to confine participatory democratic behaviour to local institutions with major political decision-making being seen as the legitimate responsibility of a representative democracy without questioning the interest at work in this.

(vi) *the citizen and the law* (p. 8), which, although it includes questions of freedoms and rights, neglects to question, for example, how the law may operate against the interests of the poor, the disempowered and the oppressed, the relationship between the law and political interests in the creation of laws, and tensions in the law.

(vii) *work, employment and leisure* (pp. 8–9), which, although it includes reference to union activity and governmental responsibility for employment and unemployment, like the documents discussed earlier, carries an implicit message of infinite possiblity and the benefits of wealth creation in materialist and leisure activities for those who abide by the 'rules of the capitalist game';

(viii) *public services* (p. 8) which, although it includes the issue of provision of public services, neglects to question the legitimacy of public, private and voluntary services and the legitimacy of the funding of, availability of, and opportunity to access what many see as a fundamental human right.

Whilst the document recognizes that 'education for citizenship involves controversial issues upon which there is no clear consensus' (ibid., p. 14) nevertheless its emphasis on understanding a received body of knowledge neglects a fully worked critical and ethical enquiry into the issues. Citizenship education has become redefined as community responsibility to an existing order rather than as critical, participatory democracy.[7]

The content of education for citizenship as described above brims over with emancipatory potential provided that it is *interrogated* rather than simply *accepted*. How one gains access to power, how one exercises and develops one's 'voice', how one exposes, acts on, and reduces vested interests needs to receive greater coverage if a fully fledged student empowerment is sought. Further, the suppression of other areas of 'citizenship' content needs to be questioned, for example Peace Studies, Political Education, Media Education.

Figure 1.5 – Key Verbs in the Education for Citizenship Document

Key Stage	Key Verbs
KS1	Think about; cooperate; agree; discuss; listen to; explore; talk about; decide; plan
KS2	Plan; review; evaluate; investigate; survey; study; organise; identify
KS3	Choose; investigate; discuss; collect examples; identify
KS4	Plan; organise; investigate; participate in; observe; debate; discuss; find out about

In terms of pedagogical principles though there is some indication of a critical stance and frequent references to 'activities', the verbs used in the document, as with the others discussed, focus mainly on understanding and exploration (Figure 1.5).

Summary

This chapter has argued that it is in cross-curriculum themes that much of the empowering and socially transforming potential of curriculum content can lie. It is in the content of these themes that the controversial nature of values, legitimacy and interests resides. Their content was seen to articulate with the wider society, ie to have referents beyond the confines of the school. In the field of pedagogy, though active, practical and experiential approaches were celebrated nevertheless they understated the interrogative and critical requirements for developing student empowerment.

The five cross-curricular themes place an emphasis on education as an instrumental activity in the service of the economy and society. It has been suggested here that if they are to enable students to take control of their lives in a rapidly changing world then they should be supplemented by another agenda of cross-curricular themes – eg empowerment, enjoyment, the experience of success, cooperation, awareness, compassion, self-determination, freedom, creativity, the development of aesthetic and imaginative forms of expression which reflect the more intrinsic worthwhileness of education. Further, the notion of empowerment requires students to move beyond the level of *understanding* the cross-curricular themes to a *critique* of the values implicit in them, to a 'problematization' of their contents. An indication of the problematical areas of curriculum content was provided for each cross-curricular theme, indicating the agenda which ideology critique might suggest. An ability to cope with change – an essential feature of the empowered citizen of the twenty-first century – requires that citizen to have a developed critical faculty. This development requires active, experiential and problem-solving approaches to learning. Content and pedagogy need to be mutually reinforcing.

The cross-curricular themes have considerable potential for learners to contextualize discussions in their own circumstances. However, critique which builds on this needs to begin from an earlier age than given in the *Curriculum Guidance* documents. The cross-curricular themes, then, provide a foundation for empowerment which needs a fuller and more developed critical superstructure.

This chapter has indicated that in approaching curriculum planning for cross-curricular themes three important criteria must be present:

22

- the status of the themes must be elevated;
- the planning must develop adaptable, flexible, active and empowered students;
- the planning must enable students' critical faculties to be exercised and developed.

These issues require teachers to work *on* as well as to work *with* the content of the *Curriculum Guidance* documents. The very non-statutory nature of the cross-curricular themes can open up opportunities for teachers and students to address these three important criteria. Their non-statutory nature is the passport for their success.

Notes

1. Young (1971) and Bernstein (1971) demonstrate how academic, literary and formally assessed curricula enable existing power structures in society to be reproduced. Though their work is over two decades old its contemporary relevance is very striking.

2. Apple (1993a), commenting on the proposals for a national curriculum in the USA, argues that what counts as important knowledge, how it is organized, who teaches it and how it is assessed, are part of the processes of the reproduction or transformation of patterns of domination and subordination in society. See also Apple (1993b).

3. Apple (1993a) argues that a national curriculum proposed for the USA will act as a mechanism for differentiating children according to fixed norms, the derivation and legitimation of which are not opened to scrutiny.

4. The rationale of this chapter derives from Habermas's (1972) work on 'knowledge-constitutive interests'. He argues that 'technical' knowledge and 'hermeneutic' knowledge (understanding) reproduce existing power structures and interests in society. For collective empowerment in society to take place then the 'emancipatory interest' must be addressed. This latter requires participants to question and critique the legitimacy of interests and power groups in society, exposing dominant values which serve to disempower sections of society. Exposing inequalities of power and illegitimate interests is the foundation for a new egalitarianism. An example of this theory translated into curriculum terms can be seen in Grundy (1987). This also draws on the literature of the sociology of knowledge (eg Young, 1971; Apple, 1990, 1993a, 1993b) which attempts to show the links that exist between ideology, interests, power, school knowledge and the reproduction of society and inequality within it.

5. This echoes Alexander's (1992) view that many views of 'good primary practice' are framed in over-minimalist or selective views such that few would disagree with them but that this masks the need for a complete statement of a full set of values (Alexander, 1992, p. 181).

6. One is reminded of Read's (1958) comments on essentialist versus contextualist art. Essentialist art is art for itself; contextualist art fulfils an instrumental function. In the *Curriculum Guidance* document here art is contextualist. If one considers that affective, artistic areas of the curriculum are accorded less status than other subjects in the national curriculum then the redefining of the arts as a service industry in education for economic and industrial understanding can be seen as an attempt to raise the status of education for economic and industrial understanding.

7. Dewey (1954) argues that a democracy should be a community in the making, always incomplete and always founded on possibility.

CHAPTER TWO

The Cross-Curricular Themes as Curriculum Statements

Introduction

Pressed with the demands of implementing the changing statutory elements of the national curriculum many teachers have placed the development of the non-statutory elements in abeyance. The documentation of the core and foundation subjects has enabled teachers to plan curricula fully and completely. However the documentation of the cross-curricular themes has been far less easy to handle. It takes the form of slender booklets of suggestions from the National Curriculum Council. Though these suggestions are helpful and interesting nevertheless they provide incomplete and uneven coverage of key elements of curriculum planning. This chapter sets out the main elements of a curriculum plan and then examines the extent to which the *Curriculum Guidance* documents address these elements, singly and severally.

Elements of a curriculum statement

One can draw on the work of curriculum planners and theorists from the middle twentieth century (cf Tyler, 1949; Taba, 1962; Wheeler, 1967; Kerr, 1968) to indicate that a curriculum statement must include reference to *aims* and *objectives, syllabus content,* the *organization* and *structuring* of the content, *teaching and learning styles* and *evaluation.* Here one begins with a statement of aims and objectives which, in turn, suggests the syllabus content most fitting to the achievement of these aims and objectives. Having decided the curriculum content the curriculum developer then looks at the most appropriate way of structuring and sequencing the content and the most suitable teaching and learning styles to 'deliver' that content. Finally, having already specified the objectives of the curricula (usually in behavioural form) the task of assessment and evaluation comprises measuring the students' achievement of the objectives.

The linearity of this pattern of development was broken by later writers (eg Skilbeck 1984; Morrison and Ridley, 1988) in two significant ways. *Firstly* they suggested that it was unnecessary to adopt such a sequenced approach to curriculum building, ie a curriculum could be built in any order provided that it included these elements. *Secondly* they acknowledged that a curriculum was embedded in the specific contexts of schools. Curriculum planners, therefore, should identify the major and minor factors, currents and constraints in the school at a given time and place and build curricula which address these factors. In short, they should provide a *situational analysis* of the curriculum in schools. This also includes a statement of the *rationale* and purposes of the curriculum.[1]

The analysis of the characteristics of the content of curricula was set out by HMI (DES, 1985) who indicated that their several and single elements should bear the hallmarks of *breadth, balance,[2] continuity, progression, relevance, differentiation and coherence.* They suggested that contents of the curriculum should identify the knowledge, concepts, skills and attitudes which the curriculum would develop. Subsequently this was developed by the National Curriculum Council in their delineation of the content and sequencing of the core and foundation subjects of the national curriculum and the *assessment* of pupils' achievements of these. This was reinforced in 1993 by OFSTED's *Handbook for the Inspection of Schools* where it indicates that some focuses of inspection would be the quality and range of the curriculum together with equality of opportunity to an entitlement curriculum.

A further element of the curriculum is the need to address *curriculum renewal, change and innovation.* This includes attention not only to content but to people; change and innovation are premised as much on interpersonal factors as they are on curriculum knowlege. This strand of curriculum building suggests that curriculum development should include significant reference to the *management* of curriculum development and innovation.

Further, a recent trend in curriculum building has been to identify how curriculum development, implementation and improvement can be managed by making them part of a *school development plan* (OFSTED, 1993). In curriculum terms this includes several features: an audit of existing work and planning beyond the next school or financial year; implementation and monitoring of plans; working relationships;

communication with and among staff, parents, pupils, community; school self-evaluation and analysis of its own performance (OFSTED, 1993). This provides a means of putting into practice the curriculum planning which schools are undertaking.

The elements identified so far comprise the formal curriculum. However there is also a need to address the *hidden curriculum*. Much work in the field of gender, racial and social class stereotypes has focused on the implicit, sometimes subliminal messages that children receive through the hidden curriculum which can be as strong as, if not stronger than, the messages of the formal curriculum.

One can draw together all of these elements and identify the key elements which should be included in curriculum building, referring specifically to the cross-curricular themes:

- a situational analysis (the context of curricula);
- a rationale for the curriculum;
- a statement of curriculum aims;
- a statement of curriculum objectives;
- a statement of how the characteristics of the curriculum have been addressed;
- an identification of the relationship between the cross-curricular themes and the national curriculum;
- a statement of the curriculum content to be included, its sequence, organization and resourcing (including time, space, materials, staff, administration, money);
- a statement of appropriate teaching and learning styles for cross-curricular themes;
- an identification of the aspects of the hidden curriculum which are addressed through the purposes, content and pedagogy of the cross-curricular themes;
- an identification of how assessment, evaluation, recording and reporting of the cross-curricular themes will take place;
- an identification of the management of the development, implementation and evaluation of the cross-curricular themes;
- an audit of existing practices and a statement of the changes and innovations which are necessary to plan, deliver and evaluate the cross-curricular themes;
- an identification of how the development of cross-curricular themes can become part of a school development plan.

A full curriculum plan or proposal should provide guidance on all of these elements. This list accords well with the framework for curriculum inspection set out by OFSTED (1993) which can be distilled into nine major elements: (i) standards of teaching; (ii) quality of learning; (iii) quality of teaching; (iv) assessment, recording and reporting; (v) the curriculum; (vi) management and administration; (vii) resources and their management; (viii) pupils' welfare and guidance; (ix) links with parents and other institutions. Subsequent chapters here address these elements of the framework.

The *Curriculum Guidance* documents as curriculum statements

When one examines the *Curriculum Guidance* documents for cross-curricular issues from the National Curriculum Council it is very plain to see that they do not address all of these elements. How can this be demonstrated? It is possible to construct a matrix of key elements of a curriculum plan and then map onto this the five cross-curricular themes, indicating which elements of the matrix are covered in the *Curriculum Guidance* documents, see Figure 2.1.

The matrix shown has in this Figure been organised so that it presents the key elements of a curriculum plan with additional detail where appropriate. It has been ordered into clusters of related items for each theme: Education for Economic and Industrial Understanding (EIU); Health Education (HLTH); Careers Education and Guidance (CEG; Environmental Education (ENV); Education for Citizenship (CTZ). Matrix planning reveals at a glance the areas which are well served by the *Curriculum Guidance* documents, those which are included slightly and those which are not included at all in the *Curriculum Guidance* documents.

The matrix indicates a very patchy coverage of the key areas of curriculum building within and between the five documents. There is little parity across the documents; each has its own emphases and de-emphases. One can total the figures at the foot of each column and aggregate each theme's percentages into totals across all of the themes. This reveals that, taking all of the themes together, high coverage of an element (●) occurs in only 39 per cent of cases; minor coverage (+) of an element occurs in only 42 per cent of cases, and no coverage at all occurs in 18 per cent of cases. The evidence of neglect, therefore, is very stark.

One can gain further information from the matrix by looking at specific rows and specific columns. One can look for generally high, medium or no real coverage and assess how even is the coverage of items.

With reference to *rows* one can see that those areas which are covered most fully were items (2), (3) and (5). Those areas which receive medium

Figure 2.1 – Key Elements of a Curriculum Plan

REQUIREMENTS OF EACH CROSS-CURRICULAR THEME					
	EIU	HLTH	CEG	ENV	CTZ
1. Context: situational analysis	+	•		•	•
2. Rationale	+	•	•	•	•
3. Aims	+	•	•	•	•
4. Objectives	•	•		•	•
5. Curriculum characteristics	•	•	•	+	•
6. Relationship to national curriculum:					
• core subjects	•	•	•	+	+
• foundation subjects	+	•	•	+	+
• PSE	+	+	+		•
• RE	+				+
• other cross-curricular elements	+	+	+	+	•
7. Components of curriculum content:					
• knowledge and understanding	•	•	•	+	+
• attitudes and values	•	•	•	+	+
• skills	•	•	•	+	+
• key concepts	•	•		+	+
• hidden curriculum		•			+
• key areas of study	•	•		+	+
• specificity of delineation	+		•	+	+
• reference to key stages	•	•	•	+	•
• prioritising of emphases		•			+
8. Pedagogy and implementation:					
• structure and organisation	+	•	•	•	+
• time and timetabling	+	•	+	+	
• teaching and learning styles		•	+	+	
• resource organization			+	+	
• methods of delivery		•	•	•	+
• using out-of-school contacts	•	+	•	•	+
9. Specific activities and experiences	•	+	•	+	•
10. Assessment, evaluation, recording			+	+	+
11. Change and innovation	+		+	+	+
12. Management issues	•	+	+	+	+
13. Whole-school policy and approach	+	•	+	+	+
14. School development planning	+	+		•	+
Covered in a major way (•)	37.5%	65.6%	46.9%	25.0%	21.9%
Covered in a minor way (+)	40.6%	18.8%	28.1%	62.5%	59.4%
Not covered at all (left blank)	21.9%	15.6%	25.0%	12.5%	12.5%
Total major coverage (•) = 39%					
Total minor coverage (+) = 42%					
Total nil coverage (blanks) = 18%					

coverage generally are items (7), (9), (12) and (13). Those areas which receive least coverage are parts of items (6), (7) and (8). It is noticeable that generally the documents do provide statements of aims and objectives and reference to the core and foundation subjects of the national curriculum. They delineate some content with reference to key stages and make some references to structure, organization and referents in the wider society beyond school. They provide examples of activities and references to the need to *manage* the implementation of the themes, commenting on the need for whole-school approaches to planning and implementation. However the documents provide very limited guidance on non-core and non-foundation curricula and are scant in their reference to the hidden curriculum. Further, they neglect to comment on resourcing, assessment, evaluation and recording. One can remark that on key areas which give rise to anxiety and concern by teachers who are implementing the national curriculum – resourcing, assessment and identifying priorities – the documents are almost silent.

One can see uneven and disparate coverage of items (1), (6), (8), (10), (11) and (14), a more even coverage of items (2), (3), (4), (5), (9), (12) and (13), and a general (if limited) coverage of item (7). One can remark here that, again, on key areas which give rise to anxiety and concern by teachers who are implementing the national curriculum – relationships between the cross-curricular themes and statutory national curriculum subjects, curriculum content, teaching styles and issues in planning and implementing the themes – the documents are patchy. The matrix indicates an interesting anomaly in that *Curriculum Guidance 3* indicated the value of making the cross-curricular themes elements of a PSE programme and yet the subsequent *Curriculum Guidance* documents provide sparse coverage of how this might be approached.

It is interesting to note that on aims and rationales the documents are very prescriptive. This conforms to the prescriptive nature of the core and foundation subjects, a feature observed in chapter one where it was indicated that there was a suppression of challenge to the national curriculum. Chapter one also indicated that the national curriculum was highly controlled and controlling and possessed limited potential for students and teachers to interrogate, critique or challenge curricula or the issues in them.

With reference to *columns* – specific themes themselves – one can observe disparate coverage of items. The fullest coverage *in depth* of all of the elements of a curriculum statement (●) can be found in the theme of *Health Education*; at the opposite pole the theme with the least in-depth coverage is *Education for Citizenship,* very closely followed by *Environmental Education*. The theme which demonstrates the greatest number of empty cells in the matrix is *Careers Education and Guidance,* very closely followed by *Education for Economic and Industrial Understanding.* The themes which demonstrate the lowest number of empty cells are *Environmental Education* and *Education for Citizenship.* The theme which demonstrates the highest number of minor coverage of elements (+) is *Environmental Education,* followed very closely by *Citizenship Education.* The theme which demonstrates the lowest number of medium coverage of elements is *Health Education.* Overall the generally most developed guidance for a full curriculum statement can be found in the *Health Education* document, whilst the generally least developed guidance for a full curriculum statement can be found in the document *Education for Citizenship.*

With reference to specific themes the document *Education for Economic and Industrial Understanding* is strong on content. However it is very weak on assessment, evaluation, recording, pedagogy and school development plans. It does demonstrate, however, some coverage of relationships to other national curriculum areas, planning, whole-school policies and examples of activities.

The document *Health Education* is very strong on rationales, aims, objectives, characteristics of the curriculum and content. It is weakest in assessment, evaluation, recording and resourcing. However it demonstrates some coverage of pedagogy, whole-school policies and relationships to other national curriculum areas.

The document *Careers Education and Guidance* is generally very patchy. It is strong on rationales and aims and provides several examples of activities and pedagogy. It is weak on reference to school development plans though it does provide some coverage of relations with other national curriculum areas, assessment and whole-school policies. Its delineation of content is polarised, being strong on knowledge, attitudes, skills and reference to key stages but silent on hidden curricula and key areas of study. This document seems to have identified very high and very low priorities with little in-between.

The document *Environmental Education,* too, is a very patchy document. It is very strong on rationales, aims, objectives and school development plans but is very weak on relationships to other areas of the national curriculum. It provides some coverage of specific activities, curriculum content, assessment, evaluation and management. What characterises this document is its overall coverage though much of this is not in depth.

The document *Education for Citizenship* is very strong on contexts, rationales, aims, objectives and examples of activities. It is weak on pedagogy and implementation. It provides some coverage of the remaining curriculum areas. This document is characterised not only by its patchiness but its lack of depth in very many important areas.

This analysis of the coverage of elements of the themes indicates their strengths and weaknesses, enabling curriculum planners to identify where their attention might have to be targeted in developing a complete coverage of a curriculum statement. However, such an analysis can offer more than simply this; it also enables a comparative analysis of clusters of issues in the curriculum to be undertaken. Where elements of the curriculum are only poorly or patchily covered in some of the *Curriculum Guidance* documents the curriculum planner, by scanning across the columns, can identify those documents where the required analysis is fuller. She can then go to those documents for examples of how to address these areas in order to provide a fuller analysis.

For example, items (1) to (5) cover contexts, rationales, aims, objectives and characteristics of the curriculum. The strongest examples of these are in the two documents *Health Education* and *Education for Citizenship*. Item (6) – relationship to other elements of the national curriculum – is best exemplified by the documents *Health Education* and *Careers Education and Guidance*. Item (7) – statements of curriculum content – is covered most fully in the document *Health Education* with an even, if not detailed, coverage indicated in the document *Education for Citizenship*. Item (8) is covered most fully in the documents *Environmental Education,* and *Careers Education and Guidance,* with *Health Education* close behind. All the documents provide examples of activities, management suggestions and reference to whole-school policies. Assessment, evaluation and recording are generally poorly covered though the documents *Careers Education and Guidance, Environmental Education* and *Education for Citizenship* provide some undeveloped guidance here. These three documents, together with *Education for Economic and industrial Understanding* also provide some limited indication of how to approach innovation and change necessary to introduce these themes. The document *Environmental Education* provides the greatest guidance on relationships to school development plans.

Summary

Matrix analysis has been adopted here as a useful shorthand means of introducing a curriculum analysis. Clearly its abbreviated nature belies the complexity of the elements and their inter-relationships. Given that time is a shortage commodity in schools, matrix analysis enables a quick identification of displayed elements to be undertaken. It affords teachers the opportunity to digest and represent significant factors which will feature in the planning of the cross-curricular themes. These factors are also important foci for the inspection of schools.

There are several key points which the preceding discussion has exposed:

- matrix analysis is a useful way of identifying the strengths and weaknesses of the *Curriculum Guidance* documents;
- matrix analysis exposes strengths, weaknesses, coverage and comparative coverage of key elements in the *Curriculum Guidance* document at a glance;
- matrix analysis identifies for planners where examples of in-depth coverage of issues might be found;
- none of the *Curriculum Guidance* documents is adequate as a complete curriculum statement;
- the incidence of in-depth coverage of elements is less that that of moderate coverage of elements in the *Curriculum Guidance* documents;
- in the *Curriculum Guidance* documents the incidence of in-depth coverage of elements is less than 39 per cent; the incidence of minor coverage of elements (the highest number) is 42 per cent; the incidence of no coverage of elements is unacceptably high at 18 per cent;
- the *Curriculum Guidance* documents are heavily prescriptive of rationales, aims and objectives;
- there is a significant silence in the *Curriculum Guidance* documents on key areas of concern for teachers – resourcing, assessment, prioritising, relationships with statutory elements of the national curriculum, planning issues;
- there is very limited parity of coverage of elements of a curriculum in the *Curriculum Guidance* documents (it is as though the teams working on these themes had no common agenda or frameworks);
- there is a marked diversity of emphases within and between the *Curriculum Guidance* documents;
- the *Curriculum Guidance* documents reinforce the notion that cross-curriculum themes can and should be part of a school development plan;
- in terms of overall coverage the fullest *Curriculum Guidance* document is that for *Health Education;* the least coverage overall is the document *Education for Citizenship;*
- all of the *Curriculum Guidance* documents recognise the need for the introduction and implementation of the cross-curricular

themes to be rooted in a whole-school approach to policy making and innovation. *Managing* the introduction of the themes requires careful and extended involvement of a whole school staff.

What emerges from the preceding analysis is that curriculum planners cannot rely on the *Curriculum Guidance* documents alone to provide adequate curriculum guidance. Their guidance is incomplete and generally under-developed. Hence in approaching curriculum development for cross-curricular themes one of the early tasks will be to develop a full curriculum statement for each theme. This will be able to feed into a school development plan and prepare schools for the requirements of formal school inspections. A curriculum statement will draw upon and augment the material from the *Curriculum Guidance* documents. Planners will have to decide the level of detail to include and the focuses of attention and prescription to be addressed.

In addition to this the message from the *Curriculum Guidance* documents points to the need for team approaches to be adopted for the planning, co-ordination and implementation of the cross-curricular themes. This derives from the suggestion that whole-school approaches and policies need to be developed. Indeed the DES project on school development plans (DES, 1989; Hargreaves and Hopkins, 1991) argues that this is a requirement of school development plans. Involving the whole staff builds in ownership and opens up channels of communication between staff which, as will be argued in chapters six and seven, are key criteria of positive organisational health and a supportive organisational climate. These are both requisites for effective innovation. The full implications of this view will be taken up in chapters six and seven. What this chapter has suggested is that the development of a full curriculum statement will not only clarify the territory of the cross-curriculum themes but, itself, will be a means of drawing together staff into teams with a common focus and purpose. The literature on school effectiveness (eg Rutter, 1979; Mortimore, 1988; Alexander, 1992; Alexander, Rose and Woodhead, 1992) suggests that an effective school is one where concerted and consistent policies are developed and implemented. The development of a full curriculum statement exemplifies this view.

Notes

1. Alexander (1992), for example suggests that 'good practice' will involve balancing empirical, conceptual, value, political, pragmatic imperatives about several features: context (physical, interpersonal), content, pedagogy, management, children, society and knowledge (pp. 179–187).

2. Alexander (1992) suggests tht this should be interpreted widely to cover: resources, management, timetabling, classroom organization, INSET, planning, and pupil-teacher interaction.

CHAPTER THREE

Approaches to Planning Cross-Curricular Themes

Introduction

This chapter concerns the planning of curriculum *content* of the cross-curricular themes both *per se* and with the core and foundation subjects. The task is to suggest ways in which the cross-curricular themes can be integrated into the timetable of the school and the core and foundation subjects. It was indicated in chapter two that it appeared that the cross-curricular themes did not work to a common agenda or have similar frameworks. The core and foundation subjects for the most part trade in attainment targets and levels of attainment, with statements of attainment within each level (with exceptions, eg Physical Education, Art and Music). This pattern is not replicated in the cross-curricular themes, which are ordered by Key Stage rather than by level. In one sense this is an attraction in that the curriculum planner can exercise a measure of flexibility within a Key Stage rather than having to adhere to a rigid 10-step ladder of objectives.

The notion of 'delivering' the cross-curricular themes is ambiguous, for it relates (a) to the organization, structure and sequencing of content, (b) to the teaching and learning styles involved in implementing the themes and (c) to timetabling. This chapter does not address the teaching and learning styles involved in implementing the themes; that is the subject of chapter four, though clearly the relationship between content and pedagogy is strong. This chapter identifies a set of criteria which must be addressed in planning the content of the themes. It then provides six approaches to planning the organization of the content of the themes in such a way that they address the criteria:

- objectives-based planning;
- using matrix planning;
- using key concepts in a spiral curriculum;

- planning by key questions;
- planning by topics;
- planning for each cross-curricular theme *per se*.

These approaches are not mutually exclusive in practice even though they are dealt with as being conceptually discrete in the discussion here.

The strengths and weaknesses of each approach are outlined and the suggestion is made that planning will draw on all of these approaches. The chapter indicates a sequence of events which curriculum developers might follow in organizing the planning of the themes and provides worked examples of how the planning of content might proceed.

Criteria for evaluating approaches to planning

The cross-curricular themes require the injection of new, additional content into school syllabuses (Morrison, 1992). Hence manageability of planning becomes a significant issue (cf Hargreaves, 1991).

Research was carried out at the University of Durham (Morrison, 1992) to see where the core and foundation subjects of the national curriculum in their existing specification already cover the content of the cross-curricular themes. A detailed exercise was undertaken which systematically mapped every knowledge aspect of the cross-curricular themes onto all the core and foundation subjects. This was undertaken to see whether, if teachers taught the core and foundation subjects, they would automatically cover the cross-curricular themes. The results are quite dramatic. They indicate that it is overwhelmingly the case that the core and foundation subjects of the national curriculum as they currently stand *do not include* the subject matter of the cross-curricular themes, therefore in their current state the core and foundation subjects cannot be relied upon to deliver the content of the cross-curricular themes. There can be little doubt that unless teachers regard the cross-curricular themes as statements of *additional* syllabus content then they will not be taught in the curriculum. It is unrealistic to pretend that making cross-curricular themes genuinely cross-curricular will not take curriculum time from other areas − subjects − of the curriculum. Hence time management becomes an integral feature of the planning of cross-curricular themes.

Knight (1991) argues that time management will need to consider four characteristics of school time: its quantity, structure, quality and flexibility. If the use of school time is to be maximised then curriculum planners will need to clarify the *quantity* of time for teaching specific curriculum areas and the most advantageous ways of organizing the time (*structure* of time).

In relation to the *quality* of time an identification of premium time is required. There is a mythology in schools that the early part of the day, week and term is the most productive as students are fresh, motivated and open to learning at these times.

The concept of *flexibility* of time suggests that times can be rearranged in schools reasonably easily. This is a feature which is more possible in primary and small schools than in secondary and larger schools. Clearly, altering the use of time in one area of the school, curriculum and group of students has a 'knock-on' effect on other areas of the school, curricula and students. However, schools are increasingly moving to flexible learning strategies (Eraut *et al*, 1991), though the rapidity of such developments is contingent upon resources in the school. The concept of *flexibility* in organizing time also requires a recognition that teachers' and students' time is differentially flexible. What might make for greater flexibility of student time might reduce the flexibility of teachers' time and *vice versa.*[1] The notion of flexibility in allocating time suggests a freeing-up of timetabling in schools which might be impracticable though desirable.

In evaluating the effectiveness of approaches to the planning of cross-curricular content, then, the issues of time managment and the maximisation of time for learning are crucial criteria.

To maximise the use of time Knight (1991) argues that teachers might increase the time available, decrease the curriculum content and speed up the learning process. This will require attention to the *length* of teaching blocks, a *prioritisation* of key concepts and curricular knowledge, skills and attitudes, and attention to *learning processes, learning theories* and *developmental psychology* respectively.

It was argued in chapter one that one of the difficulties of the cross-curricular themes is their low status. They are non-statutory, not assessed and marginalised as part of Personal and Social Education (PSE) lessons (ie those lessons which, in many secondary schools, are taught by non-specialists). Further, it is often the case that nobody has clear responsibility for developing them through the school. Hence if the full potential of the cross-curricular themes is to be realised then an elevation of their status will be required.

Elevating the status of cross-curricular themes will have to be an outcome and feature of the planning. This can be attained through several means:

● by making them visible in the curriculum − either through allotting specific time to them *per se* or signalling very clearly to staff and students where they occur as parts of other aspects of the curriculum;

- by bringing them out of PSE programmes;
- by making them free-standing with their own timetabled time;
- by attaching them to high status subjects;
- by assigning the responsibility for their development to a senior member of the school who gives it a high priority;
- by making them part of the formal assessment of students' progress;
- by using team approaches to developing and implementing the themes (discussed in chapters six and seven).

In summary, there are six important criteria to be considered in planning the content of the cross-curricular themes:

- they will need to address coherence and manageability within and between themselves and the core and foundation subjects of the national curriculum;
- their status will need to be elevated;
- though they have their own, additional, content they will need to integrate with other curriculum areas;
- attention to time management will be necessary in their planning;
- the flexibility afforded by the delineation of content, skills and attitudes in terms of key stages rather than in a 10 level sequence should be preserved in the overall planning of the themes;
- progression and continuity will have to be addressed within each theme.

Each of the six approaches to planning will be outlined and evaluated in light of these criteria.

Objectives-based planning of cross-curricular themes

A curriculum needs objectives. Yet mention objectives to many curriculum planners and they recoil, believing that what is implied is a series of behavioural objectives which render students passive recipients of predetermined curricula, which pigeonhole behaviours into low order, medium order and high order, which trivialise education and reduce it to training, which fail to capture the essence of aesthetic or emotional development, and so on through a catalogue of ills.

This section will not rehearse the argument for and against behavioural objectives.[2] It needs to be made clear that objectives are not all behavioural; they can simply be statements of intent, purposes, goals and open-ended delineations of areas of study. Indeed one could argue that a curriculum which does not know or declare where it is going risks wasting time. It might fail to address progression and continuity. It might debar forward planning and whole-school approaches to curriculum planning. In short, the curriculum might become a series of disconnected experiences, the value of which is open to question. Hence to argue for objectives-based planning is to argue that curricula should serve purposes and that the purposes should be known. That seems innocuous.

The *Curriculum Guidance* documents cast objectives clearly as statements of intent. This is much more open-ended than many of the objectives – attainment targets – of other parts of the national curriculum. The statements of objectives in the *Curriculum Guidance* documents are useful in three principal ways:

- they delineate a field of study;
- they suggest how that field might be approached;
- they suggest how progression and continuity might be developed in that field.

The first two of these are demonstrated clearly in the document *Education for Citizenship* where eight main areas of study are identified but which are prefaced by open-ended statements. For example, in the area of *The Family* the document begins:

> Pupils' experiences and appreciation of family is varied. This component encourages pupils to understand the nature of family life in all its forms and to distinguish myths and stereotypes from reality. It helps them to examine their current roles, to anticipate future roles as partners and parents and to become more effective in their relationships. (NCC, 1990f, p. 7.)

Here the field of study is defined: the family. Sub-fields are then ouglined: types of family; behaviours in families; stereotypes in discussing families; examining oneself in terms of family membership; understanding relationships; aspects of parenting. The terminology is open-ended: 'appreciate, understand, distinguish, examine, anticipate, become effective'. Rather than describing behaviours or finite outcomes, they are signposts.

The third of the three ways in which objectives are used in the *Curriculum Guidance* documents – addressing progression and continuity – is exemplified well in the document *Careers Education and Guidance* where five main elements (career, work, transition, roles and self) are set out through the key stages, with objectives identified for each. By going through the document it is a straightforward exercise to put together the objectives for each element for each key stage. An example of this can be presented as in Figure 3.1.

Figure 3.1 – Objectives for Self in Careers Education

OBJECTIVES FOR SELF IN THE DOCUMENT CAREERS EDUCATION AND GUIDANCE	
SELF	**Objective**
KS1	To begin to form an impression of self
KS2	To review personal experiences as a basis for setting new targets; To recognise and respond constructively to discrimination against certain social groups
KS3	To strengthen knowledge of self; To participate in decision-making that requires their own and other people's points-of-view to be taken into account; To explore the careers/experience of work of individuals admired by pupils
KS4	To strengthen understanding of the qualities required for team work; To prepare for situations in adult working life where negotiation and assertiveness may be required; To prepare for choices of education, training or employment post 16

In the case of *Careers Education and Guidance* the objectives can be taken from the headings in the document. In the case of *Education for Economic and Industrial Understanding* one has to look more closely to find progression and continuity. For example in key stage 1 one objective is to 'identify and make decisions about resources' which leads to the objective in key stage 2 to 'understand some of the implications of limited resources'. In key stage 3 this is developed into: 'scarcity of available resources means that decisions have to be made about how resources are used,' and in key stage 4 it appears as the statement: 'scarcity of resources means that carefully considered choices have to be made between alternative uses.' One can see here a spiral curriculum operating (discussed in more detail later in this chapter). The document Education for Economic and Industrial Understanding numbers all of its objectives for each key stage; this enables a matrix of development of objectives to be identified and presented as in Figure 3.2.

The planner can see how the objectives are developed through the key

Figure 3.2 – A Spiral of Objectives in the EIU Document

A SPIRAL OF OBJECTIVES IN THE EIU DOCUMENT				
	KS1	KS2	KS3	KS4
Objective	1	1	1	1
Number:	2	3	13, 14, 19, 20	13, 14, 19, 20
	3	4	4	4
	4	5	14	14
	5	6	3	3
	6	7	10, 11	9, 11, 12
	7	8	8	8
	8	9, 10	10, 11	9, 11, 12
	9	11, 12	5	5, 10
		2,	2, 7	2, 7
		10	10, 11	9, 11, 12
		12	5	5, 10
		13	16	17
		14	6, 16, 18	6, 17, 19
			9	7
			12	9, 11, 12
			15	13, 15
			17	18
				16

stages by reading across the rows. It can be seen in this table also where each stage after key stage 1 introduces its own additional objectives.

The least specific sets of objectives are presented in the document *Environmental Education*. The other four documents, with different degrees of accessibility, provide a set of objectives which can be put into a sequence of key stages.

The curriculum planner who wishes to use objectives as signposts will find that the *Curriculum Guidance* documents are helpful without being over-prescriptive. The planner will have to establish links between the objectives set out in the *Curriculum Guidance* documents and the other national curriculum subject documents. Identifying a spiral of objectives also provides a spine to planning with the effect of distinguishing important elements from the less important. This can address the issue of economies of timetabled time. However, given the comments earlier that the cross-curricular themes concern additional content, the saving of time might be relative rather than absolute.

Finally, it can be seen that whilst objectives-based planning fulfils several of the criteria for evaluating planning approaches, this approach does not address the elevation of the status of the cross-curricular themes.

Matrix planning of cross-curricular themes

The notion of matrix planning was introduced in the last chapter as a shorthand way of mapping curriculum coverage. Embarking on matrix planning can be to go down a road to a degree of specificity and detail which is both overwhelming and unnecessary. Hence the curriculum planner must be sensible in identifying the cut-off point in matrix planning: too much detail is superfluous, too little detail renders the matrix useless.

With that caveat it is possible, nevertheless, to use a matrix approach to planning. The first, crucial step is to be quite clear on the purposes of using matrix planning, to be sure of what they *are* and *are not*. Let us not imagine that matrix planning is trouble-free. It is useful in exposing highlights, strengths and weaknesses, emphases and de-emphases in planning. On the other hand it can easily become a nightmarish exercise which gathers dust on a staffroom shelf or forms part of a school management plan which is only exhumed in anticipation of an inspection. That is a waste of time. Matrix planning is a means to an end, not an end in itself. It can be used as part of a curriculum audit which itself is part of a curriculum development plan. The attraction of this approach is that the matrix can become both a *planning* document and a document of *record*.

Figure 3.3 indicates how a key element of one cross-curricular theme – curricular *knowledge* of the topic *Soils, Rocks and Minerals* in the theme of *Environmental Education* – can be mapped onto the attainment targets (AT 1 – AT 5) and levels (1 – 10) of one national curriculum subject: Mathematics.

The planner can go to the national curriculum document for Mathematics (DES, 1991c) and identify those aspects of the relevant part of the document *Environmental Education* to see where those aspects of environmental education can sit most comfortably with the Mathematics attainment targets and levels. In Figure 3.3 the planner might decide that Soils, Rocks and Minerals fits most comfortably with work that students are doing for Attainment Target 5, levels 4 and 5. In that case she marks on the planning matrix – maybe with a cross or line – the two small boxes for AT 5, levels 4 and 5. This provides an indication of occurrence of the theme with reference to attainment targets.

Figure 3.3 – Environmental Education: Knowledge

	ENVIRONMENTAL EDUCATION Soils, Rocks and Minerals			
MATHS	KS1	KS2	KS3	KS4
AT1	1 2 3 4 5	1 2 3 4 5	1 2 3 4 5	1 2 3 4 5
	6 7 8 9 10	6 7 8 9 10	6 7 8 9 10	6 7 8 9 10
AT2	1 2 3 4 5	1 2 3 4 5	1 2 3 4 5	1 2 3 4 5
	6 7 8 9 10	6 7 8 9 10	6 7 8 9 10	6 7 8 9 10
AT3	1 2 3 4 5	1 2 3 4 5	1 2 3 4 5	1 2 3 4 5
	6 7 8 9 10	6 7 8 9 10	6 7 8 9 10	6 7 8 9 10
AT4	1 2 3 4 5	1 2 3 4 5	1 2 3 4 5	1 2 3 4 5
	6 7 8 9 10	6 7 8 9 10	6 7 8 9 10	6 7 8 9 10
AT5	1 2 3 4 5	1 2 3 4 5	1 2 3 4 5	1 2 3 4 5
	6 7 8 9 10	6 7 8 9 10	6 7 8 9 10	6 7 8 9 10

A second example – Figure 3.4 – indicates how this approach might be used in more detail with those national curriculum subjects whose attainment targets include 'strands'. In the example here one element of the *Education for Citizenship* document – The Nature of Community – is being mapped onto the national curriculum document for Science (DES, 1991d) in terms of attainment targets (AT 1 – AT 4), strands (in Roman numerals) and levels (1 – 10).

The national curriculum subjects are identified here in terms of attainment targets rather than programmes of study. This model might be undesirable or difficult to operate. For example the national curriculum for Physical Education (DES, 1992a) differentiates by key stage, preferring to keep attainment targets to end-of-key-stage statements. Moreover, the attainment targets in Figures 3.3 and 3.4 are

42

Figure 3.4 – Education for Citizenship: Knowledge

SCIENCE	EDUCATION FOR CITIZENSHIP The Nature of Community																			
	KS1					KS2					KS3					KS4				
AT1 Strand (i)	1	2	3	4	5	1	2	3	4	5	1	2	3	4	5	1	2	3	4	5
	6	7	8	9	10	6	7	8	9	10	6	7	8	9	10	6	7	8	9	10
AT1 Strand (ii)	1	2	3	4	5	1	2	3	4	5	1	2	3	4	5	1	2	3	4	5
	6	7	8	9	10	6	7	8	9	10	6	7	8	9	10	6	7	8	9	10
AT1 Strand (iii)	1	2	3	4	5	1	2	3	4	5	1	2	3	4	5	1	2	3	4	5
	6	7	8	9	10	6	7	8	9	10	6	7	8	9	10	6	7	8	9	10
AT2 Strand (i)	1	2	3	4	5	1	2	3	4	5	1	2	3	4	5	1	2	3	4	5
	6	7	8	9	10	6	7	8	9	10	6	7	8	9	10	6	7	8	9	10
AT2 Strand (ii)	1	2	3	4	5	1	2	3	4	5	1	2	3	4	5	1	2	3	4	5
	6	7	8	9	10	6	7	8	9	10	6	7	8	9	10	6	7	8	9	10
AT2 Strand (iii)	1	2	3	4	5	1	2	3	4	5	1	2	3	4	5	1	2	3	4	5
	6	7	8	9	10	6	7	8	9	10	6	7	8	9	10	6	7	8	9	10
AT2 Strand (iv)	1	2	3	4	5	1	2	3	4	5	1	2	3	4	5	1	2	3	4	5
	6	7	8	9	10	6	7	8	9	10	6	7	8	9	10	6	7	8	9	10
AT3 Strand (i)	1	2	3	4	5	1	2	3	4	5	1	2	3	4	5	1	2	3	4	5
	6	7	8	9	10	6	7	8	9	10	6	7	8	9	10	6	7	8	9	10
AT3 Strand (ii)	1	2	3	4	5	1	2	3	4	5	1	2	3	4	5	1	2	3	4	5
	6	7	8	9	10	6	7	8	9	10	6	7	8	9	10	6	7	8	9	10
AT3 Strand (iii)	1	2	3	4	5	1	2	3	4	5	1	2	3	4	5	1	2	3	4	5
	6	7	8	9	10	6	7	8	9	10	6	7	8	9	10	6	7	8	9	10
AT3 Strand (iv)	1	2	3	4	5	1	2	3	4	5	1	2	3	4	5	1	2	3	4	5
	6	7	8	9	10	6	7	8	9	10	6	7	8	9	10	6	7	8	9	10
AT4 Strand (i)	1	2	3	4	5	1	2	3	4	5	1	2	3	4	5	1	2	3	4	5
	6	7	8	9	10	6	7	8	9	10	6	7	8	9	10	6	7	8	9	10
AT4 Strand (ii)	1	2	3	4	5	1	2	3	4	5	1	2	3	4	5	1	2	3	4	5
	6	7	8	9	10	6	7	8	9	10	6	7	8	9	10	6	7	8	9	10
AT4 Strand (iii)	1	2	3	4	5	1	2	3	4	5	1	2	3	4	5	1	2	3	4	5
	6	7	8	9	10	6	7	8	9	10	6	7	8	9	10	6	7	8	9	10
AT4 Strand (iv)	1	2	3	4	5	1	2	3	4	5	1	2	3	4	5	1	2	3	4	5
	6	7	8	9	10	6	7	8	9	10	6	7	8	9	10	6	7	8	9	10
AT4 Strand (v)	1	2	3	4	5	1	2	3	4	5	1	2	3	4	5	1	2	3	4	5
	6	7	8	9	10	6	7	8	9	10	6	7	8	9	10	6	7	8	9	10

differentiated by level – 1 to 10 – and by strand (where appropriate) but do not specify individual statements of attainment within each level. Very many statements of attainment within each level of an attainment target are very different from each other. Hence a matrix might need to be constructed which includes each statement of attainment within an attainment target.

Within each topic or element of a cross-curriculum theme there are several statements which the curriculum planner might wish to isolate. Figure 3.5 provides an example of this where one aspect of Careers Education and Guidance (Transition) is being mapped onto the national curriculum for mathematics (DES, 1991c).

Figure 3.5 Careers Education and Guidance: Knowledge

	MATHS									
TRANSITION	AT 1					AT2				
KS3	1	2	3	4	5	1	2	3	4	5
	6	7	8	9	10	6	7	8	9	10
Improve skills for managing change										
Enhance self-confidence and self-esteem										
Develop a vocabulary for describing self										
Develop techniques for self-assessment										
Clarify personal points of view about events										
To prepare for curriculum choices in key stage four taking account of implications for future career opportunities										
KS4										
To prepare for choices of education, training or employment post 16										
To make personal contact with people in their work roles in the community and develop an understanding of relationships at work										
To explore future work opportunities, understand the nature and implications of possible work opportunities										
To prepare for the tasks involved in obtaining further education, training or employment										

If the approach adopted in Figure 3.5 were applied to all of the elements of each theme then, whilst it is rich in specificity, it runs the severe risk of unnecessarily pigeonholing the areas of each cross-curricular theme. The flexibility afforded by the delineation of the cross-curricular themes in terms of key stages would be lost in this approach.

To be used to fullest effect this approach would have to generate several matrices for each theme to cover:

- each specific *knowledge* component of the theme (which may include key concepts, discussed later in this chapter);
- each specific *skill* component of the theme;
- each specific *attitude* component of the theme;
- each core and foundation subject;
- each attainment target, strand and level;
- each key stage;
- each statement of attainment within a level;
- each element of a programme of study.

Calculating the number of matrices required for a full coverage of the relationship between the five themes and all of the national curriculum subjects would require, in terms of the national curriculum as it is constituted at the time of going to press, over 14,000 matrices! Clearly that is the nonsense of being a slave to detail and to matrix planning. Curriculum planners will have to decide (a) the level of specificity which they require, and (b) what the column and row headings for each matrix will be, ie planners will have to be very selective on the matrices which are being used. Matrix planning can expose general emphases and de-emphases, highlights, strengths, weaknesses and coverage in broad terms. In a specific and very detailed form it can be used as part of a targeted piece of curriculum planning within a subject. This specificity should be targeted rather than becoming a blanket approach to planning. Not only can blankets smother as well as protect but also it is difficult to distinguish what actually is underneath the blanket!

How well does matrix planning address the six criteria for building curricula which incorporate cross-curricular themes which were outlined at the start of this chapter? Although matrix planning accords some status to the cross-curricular themes by dint of *requiring* them to be addressed, this could be seen by teachers as the same sort of task as taking the daily register – entering the appropriate mark in the appropriate box. There is no guarantee that this approach will accord them status in the eyes of teachers or students. However this approach will ensure that they are taken out of PSE programmes, that they are attached to high status subjects (taken here to mean the core subjects, see chapter one). They can, therefore, become part of the formal assessments of students' achievements. Also they are built on team approaches (ie they cannot be marginalised as the responsibility of only a minority of school staff).

This approach ensures that the cross-curricular themes are integrated into the curriculum and that their additional content is built into curricula. In attending to the integration of cross-curricular themes into core and foundation subjects attention is being given to the most efficient and effective use of teaching and learning time in school. It must be acknowledged, however, that whether this will represent an absolute reduction of curriculum content is highly questionable.

Matrix planning will enable progression and continuity to be addressed as a function at the level of detail which is built into the matrix. It can be seen, then, that matrix planning addresses very fully the six criteria for curriculum building outlined previously.

A sequence of activities can be established for curriculum planners who wish to use this approach. The six stage model below is not intended to be a complete sequence, rather it clarifies the tasks which have to be done in order to produce and disseminate data (discussed in chapters six and seven).

Step One: Identify the purposes of using a matrix approach to planning.

Step Two: Decide the contents, foci and level of specificity of the matrices.

Step Three: Identify staff who will be responsible for devising and completing the matrices.

Step Four: Identify staff who will collate and analyse collated responses.

Step Five: Clarify time scales for constructing, completing and analysing the matrices.

Step Six: Clarify how the date will be disseminated and the stages of curriculum development which will proceed from this.

Matrix planning is a useful way of gathering and processing data; as such it addresses the early stages of a school development plan – an audit of existing and proposed action. This approach can be used in a division of labour, each teacher having responsibility for entering data on the matrices by themselves before the results come to a group discussion or planning.

Key concepts in a spiral curriculum

One of the difficulties of introducing cross-curricular themes is that of curriculum overload; new material will have to integrated into the curriculum. Matrix planning indicated how that integration might take place. The use of *key concepts* represents a refinement of matrix planning. It can be regarded as an attempt to distil from the detail of curricular knowledge the content priorities in the curriculum and in the cross-curricular themes specifically. Stress has been laid on the importance of *structure* in curriculum planning as a way of rationalising the curriculum and building in progression and continuity. We can add to this Bruner's (1960) much cited support for a clear structure in the curriculum for several reasons:

- it makes subjects more comprehensible;
- it makes for economical use of time;
- it facilitates memorising and recall;
- it enables links between areas of knowledge to be drawn;
- it facilitates transfer of learning;
- it provides clear links between elementary and advanced knowledge.

Planning by key concepts uses Bruner's (1960) notion of a 'spiral curriculum'. Here fundamental elements of curricular areas are identified in elementary form and then returned to in quantitatively and qualitatively more developed and deepened forms as children move through the school. This is a means of integrating cross-curricular themes with other areas of the curriculum and a means of addressing time management. It also builds in progression and continuity in curricula and prioritises the content elements of diverse curricula. Hence the use of key concepts appears to address the several criteria for curriculum building of cross-curricular themes outlined in the early part of this chapter.

The curriculum planner is assisted greatly in the identification of key concepts in the cross-curricular themes as the *Curriculum Guidance* documents not only identify the key concepts which children should meet but, in all of the five documents, use the principle of building spiral curricula through key concepts in the structure that they bring to the documents themselves. For example the document *Careers Education and Guidance* identifies the concepts of work, career, roles, transition and self as the main organising concepts throughout the four key stages. It indicates how these can be approached and developed over the eleven years of compulsory schooling.

Concepts are *abstractions,* and as such they carry both advantages and disadvantages. On the one hand their abstractness enables them to be linked to core and foundation subjects. For example the concept of *community* can draw on the cross-curricular themes thus:

Education for Economic and Industrial Understanding, in respect of involvement in local business and community enterprise projects, wealth creation in communities, membership of the European Community;

Health Education, in respect of community provision for health care, environmental aspects of health education, developing a commitment to improving health in the community;

Careers Education and Guidance, in respect of work placements, visits to local businesses – small-scale, medium-sized, national and multi-national – workplaces and careers services, talking to adults about their employment, identification of local occupations, changing employment prospects in the community;

Environmental Education, in respect of population patterns and changes, cultural aspects of the environment, the effects of societies on the environment and *vice versa,* similarities and differences between people and their use of their environments;

Education for Citizenship, in respect of membership of different communities (the local, regional, national, European, global), the structure of communities, community needs and services, the infrastructures of communities, citizens' rights, duties, freedoms and responsibilities, political systems, pluralist communities.

On the other hand the abstractness of some key concepts can be disadvantageous. Morrison and Ridley (1988) argue that some key concepts are so abstract that the links which they make across curriculum areas are so opaque and tenuous that they are frequently lost to students. For instance, the concept of *power* has completely different meanings for the historian, the social scientist, the religious education teacher, the musician, the physical education teacher, the mathematician, the scientist. Simply to bring these areas together under the label *power* can be meaningless to students – the teacher integrates curricular areas but the student does not. This suggests that teachers should select concepts which integrate knowledge in a way which is perceptible to students. This might mean the restriction of key concepts to a limited number of curriculum areas.

An example of this can be seen in Figure 3.6 where matrix planning of a key concept – *different workplaces* – instead of relating to a possible seventeen areas of the curriculum (ie the core and foundation subjects, RE, PSE, cross-curricular themes), has been related to only six areas – English, Geography (Geog.), History, Environmental Education (Envt. Ed.), Careers Education and Citizenship Education (Citzn. Ed.).

Figure 3.6 EIU: Knowledge

	EIU			
	Key Concept: Different Workplaces			
ENGLISH	KS1	KS2	KS3	KS4
AT1	1 2 3 4 5	1 2 3 4 5	1 2 3 4 5	1 2 3 4 5
	6 7 8 9 10	6 7 8 9 10	6 7 8 9 10	6 7 8 9 10
GEOG.	KS1	KS2	KS3	KS4
AT2	1 2 3 4 5	1 2 3 4 5	1 2 3 4 5	1 2 3 4 5
	6 7 8 9 10	6 7 8 9 10	6 7 8 9 10	6 7 8 9 10
AT4	1 2 3 4 5	1 2 3 4 5	1 2 3 4 5	1 2 3 4 5
	6 7 8 9 10	6 7 8 9 10	6 7 8 9 10	6 7 8 9 10
HISTORY	KS1	KS2	KS3	KS4
AT1	1 2 3 4 5	1 2 3 4 5	1 2 3 4 5	1 2 3 4 5
	6 7 8 9 10	6 7 8 9 10	6 7 8 9 10	6 7 8 9 10
AT2	1 2 3 4 5	1 2 3 4 5	1 2 3 4 5	1 2 3 4 5
	6 7 8 9 10	6 7 8 9 10	6 7 8 9 10	6 7 8 9 10
AT3	1 2 3 4 5	1 2 3 4 5	1 2 3 4 5	1 2 3 4 5
	6 7 8 9 10	6 7 8 9 10	6 7 8 9 10	6 7 8 9 10
ENVT. ED.	KS1	KS2	KS3	KS4
People and				
Communities				
CAREERS ED.	KS1	KS2	KS3	KS4
Work				
CITZN. ED.	KS1	KS2	KS3	KS4
Work, Employment and leisure				

Though key concepts are abstract they can have very concrete referents. An example of this can be seen in Figure 3.7, where the concept of *water* has been related to Science, Technology (Tech.) (DES, 1990) and Geography (Geog.).

Each cross-curricular theme, like each subject area of the curriculum, possesses its own key concepts. If a curriculum planner is going to develop curricula by using key concepts then she will have to select those key concepts which deliberately combine cross-curricular themes *and*

Figure 3.7 – Environmental Education: Knowledge

	ENVIRONMENTAL EDUCATION																			
	Key Concept: Water																			
SCIENCE	KS1					KS2					KS3					KS4				
AT1	1	2	3	4	5	1	2	3	4	5	1	2	3	4	5	1	2	3	4	5
	6	7	8	9	10	6	7	8	9	10	6	7	8	9	10	6	7	8	9	10
AT3 Strand (iv)	1	2	3	4	5	1	2	3	4	5	1	2	3	4	5	1	2	3	4	5
	6	7	8	9	10	6	7	8	9	10	6	7	8	9	10	6	7	8	9	10
TECHNOL.	KS1					KS2					KS3					KS4				
AT1	1	2	3	4	5	1	2	3	4	5	1	2	3	4	5	1	2	3	4	5
	6	7	8	9	10	6	7	8	9	10	6	7	8	9	10	6	7	8	9	10
AT2	1	2	3	4	5	1	2	3	4	5	1	2	3	4	5	1	2	3	4	5
	6	7	8	9	10	6	7	8	9	10	6	7	8	9	10	6	7	8	9	10
GEOG.	KS1					KS2					KS3					KS4				
AT3	1	2	3	4	5	1	2	3	4	5	1	2	3	4	5	1	2	3	4	5
	6	7	8	9	10	6	7	8	9	10	6	7	8	9	10	6	7	8	9	10
AT5	1	2	3	4	5	1	2	3	4	5	1	2	3	4	5	1	2	3	4	5
	6	7	8	9	10	6	7	8	9	10	6	7	8	9	10	6	7	8	9	10

the subjects of the national curriculum – the key concepts of *different workplaces* and *water* (Figures 3.6 and 3.7) provide examples of these.

The *Curriculum Guidance* documents contain literally hundreds of key concepts at various orders of abstraction and generality. The curriculum planner, then, will have to address a hierarchy of concepts, ensuring that the most specific are able to come under the umbrella of the more general. One can demonstrate this in the five *Curriculum Guidance* documents (Figures 3.8 – 3.12). Figures 3.8 – 3.12 set out for each cross-curricular theme the high, medium and low order concepts to be found in it.

Figure 3.8 – Key Concepts in the EIU Document

Key Concepts in the *EIU* Document		
High Order	**Medium Order**	**Low Order**
Economic concepts	Production, distribution, supply, demand, innovation, scarcity, competition, goods, services, exchange, trade, efficiency, wealth distribution, poverty, interdependence, exchange rate, inequality, market share, global economy	Buy, sell, choice, cost price, advertising
Business enterprise	Production costs, action plans, business forecasts, production levels, market revenue, market research	Sales, materials
Industry and the world of work	Roles, scale, relationships, motivation, human resources, management, maximisation, design, job satisfaction, rights	Decision, needs, wants, consumer, job, tools
Consumer affairs	Change, preference, services, quality control, legal rights	Money, needs, want, afford, produce, shops, factors affecting prices, public services, office
Government and society	Economic change, technological change, work organisation, regional economy, international wealth, capitalism, socialism, finite resources, European Community, national economy, industrial responsibility, conservation, sustainable economic growth	Damage to environment, business law, kinds of work, types of job

Figure 3.9 – Key Concepts in the Health Education Document

Key Concepts in the *Health Education* Document		
High Order	**Medium Order**	**Low Order**
Substance Use and Misuses	Types of medicine, legal and illegal drugs, choices, personal responsibility, distribution of drugs, safe levels, media influences, disease transmission, administering drugs	Medication, drug, medicine, tobacco, alchohol, solvent, infection, drug limits, rules for safety, effects of drugs, laws and drugs, diseases
Sex Education	Development rates, reproductive system, personal safety, living together, puberty, parenting, friends, risk, personal choices, sexual attitudes, sexually transmitted diseases, morals, consequences of sexual activity, sexual harassment, contraception, relationships	Baby, male, female, names of body parts, talking, sharing, bodily changes, attitudes, abortion, partners, marriage, divorce, separation, menopause
Family Life	Types of family, rites of passage, relationships, child-rearing, support agencies, family planning, roles, dependence and independence, self-esteem, family problems	Birth, childhood, adult, clinic, old, death, illness, violence, vaccination, hospital, dentist, immunisation, unemployment, caring for children / relatives
Safety	Danger, safe places, protection, responsible behaviour, healthy environments, safe practices	Road safety, first aid, water safety, safety rules, safety at home / school / work, medicine, tobacco, alcohol
Health-related Exercise	Exercise, energy, strength, regular, diet, stress, circulation, advantages of exercise	Bones, organs, muscles, food types, fat, specific exercises
Food and Nutrition	Variety of food, diet, food and cultures, nutrients, food biology, food production and processing, food quality, food legislation	Names of foods, food types, balanced diet, handling food, food hygiene, shopping for food, food labels, food and self-image
Personal Hygiene	Diseases, personal routines, infection, transmission, hygiene and culture, handling food, ill-health, looking after oneself,	Dentist, washing, doctor, decay, cleaning, handkerchief, food preparation, specific practices for hygiene, keeping clean
Environmental Aspects of Health Education	Types of environments, pollution, environmental care, preventative measures, attitudes to environment, ecological interdependence, balanced lifestyle, environmental legislation, malnutrition and over-consumption	Environments – home, work, urban, school, built, natural; types of disease, ways of caring for the environment, reducing specific environmental hazards (eg passive smoking), types of pollution and pollution control, laws about the environment
Psychological Aspects of Health Education	Self-esteem, handling emotions, roles and relationships, consequences of actions, friendships and loyalty, stereotyping, mental health and illness, choosing between alternatives, stress, prejudice	Specific mental illnesses, specific stereotypes, how to cooperate, how to handle different emotions, specific consequences of actions, types of self-image, controlling behaviour, making decisions, reducing, managing, preventing stress

Figure 3.10 – Key Concepts in the Careers Education Document

Key Concepts in the *Careers Education* Document		
High Order	**Medium Order**	**Low Order**
Self	Personal achievement, self-esteem, personal viewpoints, stereotypes, equal opportunities, expert help, types of work, preferences, economic value of work, skills to manage change, self-assessment, decision-making, problem-solving, teamwork, negotiation, assertiveness, work places, views of work	Jobs, specific experiences, enjoyment, personal views on events, social skills, local jobs, specific social skills, membership of organizations, handling conflict, different types of job, work choices
Roles	Different aspects of work, different roles at work, challenging stereotypes, working conditions, linking roles in a team, changing work opportunities, locations of work, negotiating skills, consequences of decisions	Job titles, tasks and roles, forms of stereotyping local work opportunities, specific working conditions and tasks
Work	Adult work roles, viewpoints on work, requirements of work, local and regional work opportunities, changing nature of work, workers' roles and conditions, asking questions about work, classifying work, social and economic value of work, changing work patterns, job satisfaction, controversial issues in work, conflicts at work, international perspectives on work	Job titles, describing roles, specific stereotypes, specific working conditions, own views on work, information about work, specific conditions of work
Transition	Changing work opportunities, variance of work with location, moving schools, cultural influences on work, self-confidence, self-assessment skills, curriculum choices, work opportunities, training and further education	Different types of work over time and location, specific types of cultural influences on work, specific coping skills, vocabulary for describing self, specific choices, work opportunities and training needs
Career	Job satisfaction, careers and work opportunities, further education training	Describing work, sources of job satisfaction and dissatisfaction, specific work opportunities, obtaining information about work, training and further education

Figure 3.11 – Key Concepts in the Environmental Education Document

Key Concepts in the *Environmental Education* Documents		
High Order	**Medium Order**	**Low Order**
Climate	Effects of climate on vegetation, effects of pollution on climate	Specific effects of climate
Soils, rocks and minerals	Resource limitation, resource management, erosion, fertility, extractive industries	Specific instances of medium order concepts
Water	Causes of water pollution, conservation and supply of water, effects of human activity on the hydrological cycles	Specific causes of water pollution, specific examples of water conservation and supply, specific examples of medium order concepts
Energy	Limited fossil fuels, energy conservation, pollution effects of energy use	Specific examples of medium order concepts
Plants and animals	Concern for living things, conserving endangered species, exploiting wild population of plants and animals, destruction of natural habitats	Specific examples of medium order concepts
People and communities	Similarities and differences between peoples and their use of environment, demographic patterns and changes, cultural aspects of environment	Specific examples of medium order concepts
Buildings, industrialization and waste	Impact of industrialization on environment, the changing built environment and causes and purposes of this, planning and designing the built environment, waste production and its management, recycling, impact of technology on environment	Specific examples of medium order concepts
Caring for the Environment	Ensuring caring use of environment, conflicting interests in environmental management	Specific examples of medium order concepts

Figure 3.12 – Key Concepts in the Citizenship Education Document

Key Concepts in the *Citizenship Education* Documents		
High Order	**Medium Order**	**Low Order**
The nature of community	Groups and communities, roles in the community, sources of authority and influence, community needs, membership of groups, infrastructures in the community	Specific examples of medium order concepts
Roles and relationships in a pluralist society	Interdependence, similarities and differences between individuals, groups, communities, prejudice, multicultural and multiethnic communities, cultural diversity	Specific examples of medium order concepts
Duties, responsibilities and rights of being a citizen	Concepts of citizenship, balancing individual and community freedoms, exercising rights and responsibilities, equal opportunities, protecting rights, responsibilities and freedoms, duties of a citizen	Specific examples of medium order concepts
The family	Importance of the family, family structures and life cycles, challenges facing families, relationships and responsibilities, media images of the family	Specific examples of medium order concepts
Democracy in action	Political systems in the present, past and in different countries, universal suffrage, roles of trade unions, associations and pressure groups, authority, representation, human rights, constitution, monarchy	Specific examples of medium order concepts
The citizen and the law	Principles of the legal system, criminal and civil law, working of the courts, obtaining legal advice, legal rights and responsibilities	Specific examples of medium order concepts
Work, Employment and leisure	Importance of work, wealth creation and leisure, types of work (including unpaid work), responsibilities in work, changing work patterns, legal responsibilities of employers and employees, training and qualifications, trades unions, equal opportunities, unemployment, government and work, costs and consequences of decisions, leisure provision and uptake	Specific examples of medium order concepts
Public services	Paying for public services, types of service provision, providing for needs, demography and services, key features of public services (local / national) welfare, profit and rights	Specific examples of medium order concepts

Just as each core and foundation subject has its own exclusive concepts and content (for example quadratic equations in mathematics) so in cross-curricular themes there are some concepts and content areas which are very particular to (though perhaps not exclusively so) the themes in question. Examples of this are the concepts of production, distribution, exchange, business enterprise in *Education for Economic and Industrial Understanding*. What is required, then, is an identification of the key concepts which are best kept separate and those which *straddle* the cross-curricular themes and the national curriculum subjects.

It is possible to identify a core of key concepts which can be found in several of the cross-curricular themes (Figure 3.13). These can become the basis of matrix planning to indicate where they are met in the core and foundation subjects.

Figure 3.13 – Key Concepts across Several Themes

KEY CONCEPTS ACROSS SEVERAL THEMES

Economic concepts; enterprise; industry; work and careers; government and society; people and communities in pluralist societies; being a citizen; the family; democracy in action; public services; images of self.

The key concepts outlined in Figure 3.13 derive from the cross-curricular themes in a straight forward manner. However there is another set of concepts which permeate and derive from the cross-curricular themes, albeit less overtly, and which can become very powerful in integrating the cross-curricular themes and the subjects of the national curriculum. The key concepts here are presented in Figure 3.14 and are more overarching and abstract than others described so far. Their greater integrative potential is bought at the price of abstraction.

Planning curricula by the use of key concepts addresses very favourably the six criteria for evaluating planning approaches set out in the early part of this chapter. By ensuring that key concepts are chosen which straddle the cross-curricular themes and the subjects of the national curriculum, the integration of the two will be achieved. Further, in deliberately avoiding planning in terms of subjects only, the

56

Figure 3.14 – Key Integrative Concepts

KEY CONCEPTS WHICH INTEGRATE
THEMES AND SUBJECTS

Causality and consequence; conflict and consensus; cultural
stability and change; similarity and difference; continuity
and change; freedom and constraint; equality and inequality;
poverty and wealth; unity and disunity; competition and
co-operation; capitalist and sociality economy; revolution
and adaptation; representative and participatory democracy;
power and legitimacy; welfare rights and provision;
independence and interdependence; infrastructures of society
and bureaucracy; societal control and social freedoms;
traditions, values and beliefs.

---

impact of the cross-curricular themes will be recognised and built into
curricula. This necessarily will require them to be taken seriously by
planners, i.e. planners necessarily will be according them status in the
curriculum.

With regard to the criterion of time management it was suggested
earlier that if an already overfull timetable was required to contain yet
more content then ways must be found to (a) decrease curriculum
content, (b) identify priority areas and issues, and (c) speed up the
learning process. Planning by key concepts addresses these three points
as it requires curriculum planners to focus on organizing principles
(seeing the wood for the trees), to make clear to students the structure of
spiral curricula so that memorisation is facilitated, and to identify the
high, medium and low order key concepts respectively. Key concepts,
then, can be used both in the planning and the delivery of the cross-
curricular themes.

It was argued in the previous section that one of the dangers of matrix
planning is that it can quickly become a runaway exercise of
pigeonholing every possible factor or feature. Here, too, a sense of
realism must pervade the approach to planning curricula by key
concepts; too specific a level of detail simply becomes counter-

productive. A sensible approach to this form of planning recognises that matrix planning for key concepts is useful in identifying the main features, the high priority or overarching key concepts, of content which can be developed in curricula.

One of the criteria for curriculum planning is that it should preserve the flexibility which inheres in the cross-curricular themes by dint of their being related to key stages rather than to levels of attainment. Planning by key concepts identifies the minimum core of curriculum content whilst enabling flexibility of interpretation and extension to be preserved. In this respect there is considerable flexibility available to planners.

The final criterion suggested earlier – the ability to address progression and continuity – goes to the very heart of planning by key concepts, for inherent in them is the requirement that they generate spiral curricula. This approach to planning is one of the most powerful ways of planning for progression and continuity. It does not stifle flexibility but, in fact, creates more room for this than do other approaches.

As with the previous approach, it is possible to identify a sequence of activities for curriculum planners who wish to adopt this approach. It is important in this not to be too directive about the level of specificity required. What will become clear as the establishing of the key concept proceeds is the level of specificity or generality of the key concepts.

Step One: Identify the purposes of using this approach to planning.
Step Two: Identify the staff who will be responsible for analysing the *Curriculum Guidance* documents to find the key concepts contained in them.
Step Three: Set time scales for the identification and listing of the key concepts from these documents.
Step Four: Pool the findings amongst the development team (the nature, constitution, purposes and tasks of this will be discussed in chapter seven), putting the key concepts into a hierarchy.
Step Five: Decide which key concepts and which level of key concepts – high order, medium order, low order – will be used in the planning.
Step Six: Identify the staff who will be responsible for devising and completing the matrices of key concepts in terms of their relationship to the subjects and other areas of the national curriculum.
Step Seven: Set timescales for completing the matrices.
Step Eight: Pool the findings amongst the development team(s) and

58

agree the steps forward in terms of *what* will be introduced, *who* will introduce it (them) and *who else* will be involved, *when* they will be introduced, *with which* students they will be introduced, *how* they will be introduced and *how* they will be evaluated.

Planning by key concepts not only helps to clear teachers' minds about the content of curricula but it avoids the overload which matrix planning outlined in the previous section risks. It has much to recommend it.

Planning by key questions

This approach uses and develops the notion of planning by key concepts. It is possible to identify a limited number of questions which teachers can use as starting points for analysing and planning the cross-curricular themes. The questions are astringent, drawing together central issues from the *Curriculum Guidance* documents and suggesting that these can be used to integrate the themes with the core and foundation subjects. It is a two-stage process: stage one involves the derivation of the 'key questions' from the key concepts of the cross-curricular themes and the *Curriculum Guidance* documents; stage two involves an indication of how those questions can be answered with reference to the cross-curricular themes and the other subjects of the national curriculum.

An interesting example of stage one can be seen in the work of Buck and Inman (1992). From an analysis of the *Curriculum Guidance* documents they identify nine questions which can be used to draw together the study of cross-curricular themes (Buck and Inman, 1992, pp. 16–35) and they indicate those sections of the *Curriculum Guidance* documents to which the questions refer:

- What is the nature of our rights and responsibilities in everyday life?
  Key concepts: rights, responsiblity, equality, inequality, interdependence.
- On what basis do people influence and control others?
  Key concepts: power, authority, equality, interdependence.
- What is the balance between individual freedom and the constraints necessary for co-operative living?
  Key concepts: freedom, constraint, rights, responsibility, welfare, health.
- In what ways do people organise, manage and control their relationships?

Key concepts: conflict, co-operation, culture, belief, equality, inequality, interdependence, technology.

- In what ways are people different and with what consequences?

  Key concepts: social differentiation, equality, colonialism, imperialism, wealth, race, gender, scarcity.

- How do people learn the requirements of a particular culture?

  Key concepts: socialisation, culture, belief, equality, inequality, power, authority.

- What constitutes a community, how are communities organised?

  Key concepts: community, interdependence, environment, representation, rights, responsibility, authority, scarcity.

- In what ways are the welfare of individuals and societies maintained?

  Key concepts: welfare, health, wealth, interdependence, rights, responsibility, equality, inequality, freedom, scarcity, choice, production, consumption.

- On what basis do people make decisions when faced with particular choices?

  Key concepts: scarcity, choice, need, want, opportunity, cost, division of labour, environment, rights, responsibility.

The list of questions and references (not included here) provides a useful introduction to the *Curriculum Guidance* documents. However the questions do not cover all aspects of the cross-curricular themes and some of the references to the documents do not indicate to which specific key stages they refer. One notices that, though the questions are open-ended and imponderable – incapable of resolution – they nevertheless require the *identification* of facts and issues. One notices that the questions deal in 'what' and 'how' but do not include 'why'. Chapter one indicated that the attraction of the cross-curricular themes was their ability to empower and to *transform* the *status quo;* the set of nine questions above, although they are open-ended, in themselves are not open-ended enough to enable students to interrogate and critique issues from the standpoint of legitimacy.

The nine questions provide a starting point for analysis though they would need to be augmented in three ways:

- by covering all aspects of the cross-curricular themes;
- by introducing 'why' questions and questions which provoke an interrogation of legitimacy and justifications for practices;
- by framing questions which not only enable the cross-curricular themes to be addressed but also enable planners to link the cross-curricular themes to the other national curriculum subjects.

As they stand the nine questions do not link with the national curriculum subjects straightforwardly, ie in terms of the criteria for evaluating approaches to curriculum planning they allow the cross-curricular themes to continue to be marginalised. They do not address progression and continuity in any developed sense, drawing on selected key stages within each question. They do not engage the whole gamut of the theme in question. They do not address the questions of time management (though, by implication, the themes would be *completely* additional to the other subjects of the national curriculum). This, however, is not necessarily a total criticism of the nine questions, for the authors are clear (ibid., p. 16) that the intention was not to address the core and foundation subjects and that the questions were simply heuristic tools rather than a finished product in curriculum building.

What is required is an indication of how planning by key questions can move from stage one – addressing the cross-curricular themes – to stage two – using questions derived from an analysis of the cross-curricular themes to integrate the themes with the core and foundation subjects. How can this second stage be addressed?

From an indication of key concepts in the cross-curricular themes their relationship to the core and foundation subjects can be identified. From here it is a relatively straightforward matter to raise questions which derive from the key concepts. For example if we wished to augment the nine questions by Buck and Inman (1992) above so that they address not only the cross-curricular themes in full but also the national curriculum subjects we could raise the following set of questions:

(i) In what areas of our lives do individuals, groups and communities exercise their rights, freedoms, duties and responsibilities as citizens? What factors bear on the exercise of such rights? How acceptable are these? What can be done to promote rights, freedoms, duties and responsibilities?

(ii) How can we prepare for life after school? Why do we need to work? Why are employment and unemployment important? What causes unemployment? How justifiable are employment and unemployment? What can be done to further employment and careers?

(iii) In what areas and for what reasons are freedom, power, control and constraint exercised at home, at school, at work and elsewhere? On what grounds can these be justified? How can freedoms, powers, controls and constraints be used to give individuals, groups, communities and nations more control over themselves?

(iv) What kinds of relationships are there at home, at school, at work, elsewhere? What is the basis of these relationships? What are the consequences of these relationships? How can relationships be managed and sustained?

(v) In what ways are individuals, groups, communities and countries similar and different? What causes these similarities and differences? How acceptable aie the similarities and differences? What can be done to promote acceptable similarities and differences?

(vi) How do individuals, groups, communities, regions, countries sustain themselves? What support structures are there for this sustenance? How can support for individual, group, community, region and national development be addressed and managed? What issues are there in providing sustenance and support? How can these be addressed?

(vii) What choices do individuals have to face as they grow older? How can they be supported in addressing these decisions? How acceptable are the factors which bear on the decisions that they have to take? How can choices be made more open, accessible and responsible?

What is made explicit in these questions is an interrogation of the *status quo* and the examination of the possibilities and mechanisms for the transformation of the *status quo*. It was argued in chapter one that acceptance of the *status quo* was not enough, that if society is both reproducing and producing itself then the substance and the manner of its evolution and transformation − the very heart of the cross-curricular themes, with their emphasis on individual, group, cultural, social and national empowerment − needs to be addressed. One can identify four stages of analysis of society (cf Smyth, 1989, 1991):

- **Stage One:** *description* and *interpretation* of existing situations, practices and circumstances;
- **Stage Two:** *analysis and interpretation* of causes of and backgrounds to these situations, practices and circumstances;
- **Stage Three:** *Setting an agenda* for action and the criteria to successful achievement of the agenda;
- **Stage Four:** *Evaluating* the achievement of the agenda.

Stage four is distinct from the other three stages in that it is formative and can only take place after a period of time has elapsed.

Evaluating this approach to planning involves addressing the six main criteria outlined at the start of this chapter. As with key concepts, *coherence and manageability* feature highly in this approach as it is strongly reductionist. In terms of *elevating the status* of the cross-curricular themes this approach to planning takes the themes out of PSE and is devolved onto team approaches to curriculum building. The key questions quite clearly *integrate the themes and the national curriculum subjects.* Planning by key questions − and their relatedness to key concepts − is an attempt to pare down to the essentials the several elements of the cross-curricular themes and their related parts of the national curriculum subjects. This addresses the criterion of *time management.* By setting out a core of questions and concepts this apprach enables a measure of *flexibility* in planning to be achieved. Finally, by basing the key questions on the key concepts of the previous section this approach enables *progression and continuity* to be addressed as they are an intrinsic requirement of a spiral curriculum which is built on key concepts.

As with the previous two approaches, a sequence of activities can be set out which enables planners to develop curricula by using key questions. It is necessary to recognise here that the key questions, as they appear here, are for curriculum planners to use rather than for students to use as they are very generalized and will require substantiation in curriculum areas. It is only in step nine that these very big questions will be broken down in specific questions which students can address. The first seven steps are very nearly a replica of the steps for planning by key concepts as it is necessary to generate these before the key questions can be addressed which derive from them; the remaining three steps deal specifically with generating and using in planning a set of key questions:

Step One: Identify the purpose of using this approach to planning.
Step Two: Identify the staff who will be responsible for analysing the *Curriculum Guidance* documents to find the key concepts contained in them.
Step Three: Set time scales for the identification and listing of the key concepts from these documents.
Step Four: Pool the findings amongst the development team (the nature, constitution, purposes and tasks of this will be discussed in chapter seven), putting the key concepts into a hierarchy of subsumption.
Step Five: Decide which key concepts and which level of key concepts − high order, medium order, low order − will be used in the planning.
Step Six: Indicate the staff who will be responsible for identifying

the key concepts in terms of their relationship to the subjects and other areas of the national curriculum.

Step Seven: Set timescales for completing step six.

Step Eight: Pool the findings and identify the key questions which arise from the key concepts choses. Ensure that the questions, though framed at a high level of generality, will enable very specific, concrete responses to be given by the development team (ie so that the answers to the questions will indicate the curriculum areas which will be addressed). Ensure also that the curriculum content on which the questions will be focused will enable objectives to be drawn up and referenced to Key Stages and curriculum areas.

Step Nine: Translate each key question into very specific questions which can be asked of *students* working in the several curriculum areas, ie operationalise the questions from the students' point of view. For each specific question indicate the curriculum areas in which they will be working.

Step Ten: Pool the findings amongst the development team(s) and agree the steps forward in terms of *what* will be introduced, *who* will introduce it (them) and *who else* will be involved, *when* they will be introduced, *with which students* they will be introduced, *how* they will be introduced, *how* they will be evaluated.

As with planning the curriculum by key concepts, planning by key questions not only helps to clear teachers' minds about the content of curricula but it avoids the overload which matrix planning outlined in the earlier section risks. Finally, it must be acknowledged that the use of key questions embodies very strongly and fully the requirement of the cross-curricular themes: that they develop in students an interrogative and critical stance towards issues, curriculum content and factors in their everyday lives. This is a very powerful argument for their use, both in the planning and delivery of the themes.

Planning by topics

A topic is eclectic, comprising a field of study which draws on several areas of the curriculum as appropriate; it establishes conceptual and content-based links between curriculum areas so that they provide a unity of experiences for the child. These links are made between several subject areas both epistemologically and psychologically so that learning and knowledge in several areas of the curriculum are mutually reinforcing. Having said this one can identify three types of topic:

- *Type One:* a topic which draws elements from different curriculum

64

Figure 3.15 – A Year's Topic Plan for a Primary School

Class	Term 1	Term 2	Term 3
Reception Class	Ourselves	Homes	People who Help Us
	Toys	My school	Water
Year 1	Clothing Weather	Light and Colour Travel	Growing Minibeasts
Year 2	Power Water	Sound The Five Senses	Animals Pollution
Year 3	Journeys Egypt	Time Greece	Flight Ourselves
Year 4	Settlers Food	Light and Colour Tudors and Stuarts	Structures Forests
Year 5	Electricity My body	Great Britain Victorian Britain	Exploration Weather
Year 6	Space Transport	Post-war Britain Planet Earth	Local Study Habitats

areas (for example a topic on *Ourselves* might draw on English, mathematics, science, geography, environmental education, citizenship education, health education, technology, etc.);

- *Type Two:* a topic which, though it can make passing references to several curriculum areas, draws mostly from only two or three main curriculum areas (for example a topic on *Rivers* might make passing reference to mathematics and history but place much greater emphasis on geography, environmental education and science);

- *Type Three:* a topic which lies within a single subject area (for example a topic on *Shape* in mathematics, or a topic on *Sex education* in health education, or a topic on *The Great Fire of London* in history.

Type one is the approach which can be found most in primary schools, type two can be found in primary and secondary schools, type three can be used to deliver themes within subject-based secondary school curricula.

In Type One and Type Two topics the approach is very straighforward and can be set out in a four stage sequence for primary schools (Ryan, 1992; Lowes, 1992):

Step One: The topics for the school year are decided right through the school (Figure 3.15) and are set out in topic webs to determine the subjects of the national curriculum which will be covered in the topics. This might embrace a whole school-topic or different topics which will be addressed by different classes through the school. At this stage progression and continuity through the national curriculum subjects will have been addressed, though not for the cross-curricular themes.

Step Two: For each topic a matrix is planned so that it is possible to see where the five cross-curricular themes can be integrated with the topics, see (Figure 3.16) which develops the topic of 'Ourselves' from Figure 3.15 (Envt. Ed. = environmental education; Citzn. ed. = education for citizenship).

Note that this is an open-ended general matrix, avoiding the problem of too much detail in matrix planning. This approach is very useful for ensuring *continuity* across the topics though, at this stage, it does not address *progression* through the topics. Each teacher completes one sheet per topic for her/his class. At this stage the topics throughout the school will have been mapped and the places where the cross-curricular themes will be addressed will have been identified. Hence in a seven teacher primary school (Reception class plus a class for each of years 1–6) there will be seven examples of Figure 3.16 for each topic. If six topics per year are addressed by each teacher then there will be six sheets per teacher.

Step Three: The task now is to address progression and continuity *within* each of the five cross-curricular themes and *within* and *between* each topic undertaken *by each class*. For this a 'scissors and paste' approach might be adopted. Each teacher extracts one cross-curricular theme from all of the year's topics and sets that cross-curricular theme in order through the year so that one sheet will contain one cross-curricular theme, eg Environmental Education, and another sheet will contain another theme etc., (Figure 3.17).

66

Figure 3.16 – Mapping Cross-curricular Themes onto Topics

	Ourselves at Home, in School and in the Local Environment
EIU	Shopping, study of local shops; awareness of value of money; buying and selling (Geog. Maths.); old shops and habits (Hist.); role play in shopping in home corner; classroom shop; different shops, supermarkets; people at work in cities (Geog.), towns, villages – comparative study of different environments
Health Ed.	Care of our bodies – personal hygiene, visit from school nurse; how to keep our bodies healthy – food, clothing, links with preventative health care – eating, sleeping, exercise (Sc.); safety – care, road safety police visit – dangers of water, electricity etc., care of teeth – visit from school dentist; learning to care for the welfare of others in school, being part of the school environment – sense of fair play – forgiveness etc. (RE)
Careers Ed.	Occupations (a) in the local environment (b) on a wider scale, eg town, city; role play situations for the work of several occupations (Geog.); What will be in the future? How do people become shop assistants, nurses, teachers etc.? People who work in our school. Work in our families – paid and unpaid work, value of stereotypes to be considered and challenged. Comparative studies of work in our families compared to parents and grandparents (Hist. and Geog.)
Envt. Ed.	Environmental features – climate, soils, rocks, minerals, water and energy (Geog.); growing in our environment – ourselves, seeds, crops, animals (Sc.); light and water, natural resources – fuels in our homes; pollution and litter around us
Citzn. Ed.	Learning to be part of the school environment; acceptable and unacceptable social behaviour; everyday life in classroom, play area, playing and learning together; role play in different situations – bullying, arguing, accidents, caring for each other in families; Jesus's teaching on citizenship and how we should live our lives (RE)

Figure 3.17 – Building Progression through One Class

YEAR FIVE – CROSS-CURRICULAR THEME: EIU	
Electricity	
My Body	
Great Britain	
Victorian Britain	
Weather	
Local Study	

Step Four: The task now is to address progression and continuity within each of the five cross-curricular themes *through the school*. For this another 'scissors and paste' approach might be adopted. Each cross-curricular theme on each sheet is extracted and re-

68

Figure 3.18 — Building Progression through the School

CAREERS EDUCATION AND GUIDANCE	
Reception Class	
Ourselves	
Homes	
People who Help Us	
Toys	
My School	
Water	
Year 1	
Clothing	
Light and Colour	
Growing	
Weather	
Travel	
Insects	
Year 2	
Power	
Sound	
Animals	
Water	
The Five Senses	
Pollution	
Year 3	
Journeys	
Time	
Flight	
Egypt	
Greece	
Ourselves	
Year 4	
Settlers	
Light and Colour	
Structures	
Food	
Tudors and Stuarts	
Forests	
Year 5	
Electricity	
Great Britain	
Exploration	
My Body	
Victorian Britain	
Weather	
Year 6	
Space	
Post-war Britain	
Local Study	
Transport	
Planet Earth	
Habitats	

ordered so that one sheet will contain one cross-curricular theme, eg Careers Education and Guidance, which is set out in order, beginning at the reception class and ascending to the Year 6 class. (Clearly this is a task which would not fit comfortably into a single side of paper as on figure 3.18 which is by way of example only; rather it could be recorded on a large A1 flip-chart size sheet of paper). The process is repeated four times, ie until the five themes are each re-ordered onto a new sheet each, for example Figure 3.18.

It is possible now to discern progression, continuity, overlap, disjunctions and absences, strengths and weaknesses, emphases and de-emphases, and to plan for any amendments needed to ensure that the cross-curricular theme demonstrates progression and continuity.

The examples given so far feature primary schools. In the case of secondary schools the Type Three topic can be adopted – where the topic is kept within a subject area. In this case a four-step sequence can be set out to plan the development of cross-curricular themes in a subject-framed curriculum. The example chosen here is for the subject of History:

Step One: Plan the introduction of cross-curricular themes for each topic in History, for each academic year and for each year of students in school, see Figure 3.19.

Step Two: Plan the year's topics and list them in the sequence in which they will be covered, setting a matrix as in Figure 3.20 and completing it in respect of each cross-curricular theme.

Step Three: Review the sheets to identify progression and continuity. In a secondary school continuity will have to be seen not only *vertically* (as in 'progression through the school year(s)') but *laterally* across the several classes of the school year. It is possible now to discern progression, continuity, overlap, disjunctions and absences, strengths and weaknesses, emphases and de-emphases, and to plan for any amendments needed to ensure that the cross-curricular theme demonstrates progression and continuity.

Step Four: At this stage the planning will move out of the History curriculum, for, if the coverage of the cross-curricular themes is to be addressed across the whole of a secondary school student's programme in any one year, attention will need to be given to the whole curriculum diet which the student experiences. Hence steps one and two will have to be undertaken by all of the relevant teachers. They will then pool their findings to see over the whole of

Figure 3.19 – Cross-curricular Themes in Secondary History

YEAR 8 – THE EARLY ROMAN EMPIRE: HISTORY	
EIU	
Health Ed.	
Careers Ed.	
Environmental Ed.	
Citizenship Ed.	

Figure 3.20 – Progression in Cross-curricular Themes in Secondary History

YEAR 8 – EDUCATION FOR CITIZENSHIP: HISTORY	
The Roman Empire	
The Roman Conquest of Britain	
Britain 1066 – 1215	
Britain 1215 – 1500	

that year's curriculum (a) where duplications, absences, progression, continuity (across teachers and across subjects) is present, (b) where items have been fully and partially covered and (c) where items have been emphasised, de-emphasised, co-ordinated or left discrete.

This activity will also enable teachers to locate in which subjects specific cross-curricular themes are most represented and in which they are least represented. The discussions then will focus on the acceptability of the representation of themes in subjects and decisions taken either to maintain or to adjust this. One can see in type one, type two and type three variants of topic work that decisions on continuity precede decisions on progression. Progression through each theme is comparatively straightforward to plan where each cross-curricular theme is dealt with separately.

Evaluating the adequacy of topic approaches in terms of the criteria established at the outset of this chapter it can be seen that the common ownership of the themes and their place in the full range of the national curriculum subjects is a means of *raising their status*. Their potential for *integration* into curriculum areas other than their own is facilitated in topic work. However this approach does create three problems which are well recognised in topic work in primary school:

- if elements of the cross-curricular themes do not fit comfortably into the national curriculum subjects and, therefore, are excluded from topics then those areas of the themes which are 'leftover' are regarded as unimportant and inessential;
- an attempt to cover all elements of the cross-curricular themes in topic work can result in items from the themes being forced into topics unfairly, ie their appearance in the topic is contrived and artificial;
- those elements of the cross-curricular themes which are not covered by topics still have to be addressed. This might mean that some of the areas of the themes have to be 'mopped up' in unrelated and underdeveloped fragments, ie the holism of the topic approach brings fragmentation in its wake.

Topic work is an attempt to make effective and efficient use of *time;* however it is far from certain that it will actually succeed in managing the timetabled time any more efficiently by reducing time spent on other curriculum subjects.

Though steps have been taken to ensure that *progression* and *continuity* are addressed in topic work recent reports on primary schooling (eg Mortimore, 1988; Alexander, 1992; Alexander *et al*, 1992) suggest that topic work is problematical:

- it risks poor matching;
- it can waste time with students simply copying out of books;
- it can be an undemanding collection of only partially related scraps of knowledge, many of which are of a low order;
- it does not enable significant and trivial knowledge to be differentiated;
- it can make for an inefficient use of teachers' time.

Hence though the benefits of topic work are well-known to primary teachers who have succeeded in motivating and challenging students and developing autonomy and responsibility in them, this approach is not without its risks. As in many walks of life, striving for high success is a high risk activity.

Planning separately for cross-curricular themes

In this approach timetabled time is devoted specifically to one or more of the cross-curricular themes. The arguments presented earlier suggested that the cross-curricular themes at heart were really extra, if covert, subjects, having their own content, concepts, structure and pedagogies. In terms of the six criteria set out at the beginning of this chapter for evaluating approaches to planning there are several important features to this approach:

- it recognises that these themes are, in fact, subjects;
- it accords them status by allotting them their own specific timetabled time rather than risking their place as bolt-on nuisances to other subjects;
- it guarantees them a place and a time on the school curriculum;
- it takes them out of low status PSE programmes;
- it makes their organization, structure, sequencing, progression and continuity infinitely more easy for teachers to plan than if they are parts of other syllabuses;
- it makes them very visible in the curriculum;
- it makes it much more realistic and easy to appoint a senior member of the school to have responsibility for their implementation, ie status is *seen to be given* to them by attaching them to a named high-level colleague;
- it enables them to be taught by specialists, again a means of raising their profile and their consequent status;
- it does not overburden all teachers with yet more curriculum development, which, in the case of cross-curricular themes, they may regard as peripheral and as a distraction from the 'real' task in hand of teaching subjects and preparing students for examinations.

However, against these several attractions there are significant and overriding anxieties about this approach:

- it violates the very principle of cross-curricularity on which the themes are premissed;

- integration with other curricular areas is rendered impossible;
- removing them from their contact with national curriculum subjects not only risks their marginalisation but might not guarantee the elevation of their status – the examples of RE, Music, PSE and Art in many schools is witness to this;
- it is unclear who will teach them. Though their isolation from the other national curriculum subjects does enable them to be taught by specialists it is not certain whether this will require new appointments to the school, a massive staff development exercise, or whether, in fact, like PSE in many schools, they will be taught by a form teacher who has no more specialist knowledge of them than her colleague next door;
- if this form of delivery were to be adopted careful timetabling would need to be undertaken so that during the year a five-theme syllabus could be taught. This would raise the question of whether the themes would be taught in parallel or one after the other. If the former were to be applied then this would either require significant blocks of time to be devoted to them or risk fragmenting timing and its related learning opportunities in order that small parts of each theme might be covered on a weekly, fortnightly, monthly or half-termly basis. If the latter were to be applied then there would be massive discontinuity of learning as themes would be begun and then left for weeks or months before being resumed. Hence the success of this approach is contingent upon the most problematic of criteria – time management. It adds a significant amount to timetabled time in a situation where this time, as many teachers will aver, is quite simply unavailable.

If this approach to cross-curricular themes is adopted, whereby they are treated like any other timetabled subject, then there is much in the *Curriculum Guidance* documents by way of examples and suggestions to provide support for teachers here. However this section, whilst presenting the case for this approach, argues that it is too problematical to be taken seriously.

Summary

This chapter has argued that an inevitable concern of planners is to have objectives. These need not be behavioural, indeed the analysis provided in this chapter indicated that in the *Curriculum Guidance* documents they were not. Objectives were necessary in order to give structure and purpose to planning. It was possible to identify a balance of openness and direction in the objectives of the *Curriculum Guidance* documents that rendered them helpful not only in indicating areas for planning, but in providing some ways in which progression could be built through the spiralling of objectives.

Matrix planning is valuable if teachers do not become obsessed with attempting to include too fine a level of detail in matrices unless specific aspects of planning require to be targeted. It was suggested that matrix planning could enable areas of emphasis and de-emphasis to be highlighted, ie this approach could have a revealing function. The approach to planning by key concepts was seen to take this a stage further. Here, using matrix analysis, a bridge could be built between the cross-curricular themes and the other national curriculum subjects. Key concepts were held up as being valuable not only for their potential economy of time but for their ability to go to the heart of subject matter in a way which would enable students to learn and memorise easily and efficiently.

The argument then suggested that if key concepts were operationalised into open-ended key questions this would enable the open-ended and transformative, empowering potential of the cross-curricular themes to be released and realised. This approach was seen as possessing fidelity to the open-endedness of the issues treated by the cross-curricular themes. It was seen also as a powerful means of developing in students an appropriately interrogative stance to controversial issues.

Given that the cross-curricular themes were an attempt to develop the 'whole' person, an approach to planning which embodied the holistic nature of development was seen to reside in topic work. Three types of topic work were identified and their utility for primary and secondary schools was indicated. Finally a suggestion that each cross-curricular theme itself should become a subject in its own right was seen to be too problematical to be supported.

No single approach can be relied upon to deliver the cross-curricular themes on its own. Each approach was seen to have its advantages and disadvantages. Hence curriculum planners will have to draw on these approaches eclectically. These approaches, in fact, are not mutually exclusive. One can take the notion of key concepts and key questions and their development through matrix planning and use these as organising principles for subject-specific or cross-subject topics; one can use a matrix approach to identify where the content of the cross-curricular themes can be integrated with the content of subjects of the national curriculum – be these framed in subject specific or cross-subject terms. One can plan where it might be more effective and more economical in terms of human, material and temporal resources to treat the subject matter of the cross-curricular themes as separate from the other subjects of the national curriculum and where it might be more effective and economical to integrate them. That is part of the planning process.

What is very clear is that it is as senseless to force the cross-curricular themes to integrate with the other subjects of the national curriculum as it is to insist that they should at all times be kept separate from the other national curriculum subjects lest they contaminate the 'important' business of disseminating academic knowledge. Between the poles of inclusiveness and exclusiveness there is a vast territory where collegial planning and curriculum development can take place. Here personal needs, interests and abilities can be met and positive working relations can be fostered. Just as the cross-curriculum themes address issues which are not open-and-shut, an approach to planning their organization and implementation in schools should be open and flexible, capable of drawing upon teachers' strengths and developing areas of expertise and interest. This serves a fundamental principle of the cross-curricular themes, *viz.* that they develop flexibility, adaptability and autonomy in students.

An eclectic and flexible approach can be managed not only by attention to *approaches* to planning the content of curricula so that they embody the cross-curricular themes, but, significantly, will have to examine the organization of teaching and learning. This includes teaching and learning styles, staff deployment and the generation of flexible teaching and learning strategies, in short to *pedagogy*. The cross-curricular themes, as will be seen, recommend their own styles of delivery and their own set of teaching and learning strategies. These, too, will have to be integrated with the subjects and pedagogies of the national curriculum. It will be argued that it is only if content and pedagogy are integrated that the criteria for evaluating planning approaches set out at the beginning of this chapter can be met. How this can be approached is the subject of the next chapter.

Notes

1. Alexander (1992) comments that the more accessible teachers make themselves to children the less time they have for extended and challenging interactions with them, and the more they move to extended and challenging interactions the less demanding will be the tasks set for the other children (p. 66).
2. This is set out clearly in Hirst (1975) and Morrison and Ridley (1988).

CHAPTER FOUR

Delivering the Cross-Curricular Themes

Introduction

The previous chapter argued that the notion of 'delivering' the cross-curricular themes embraced the organization of the curricular content, the timetabling arrangements and the teaching and learning styles to be adopted. A central concern in this process was the need to develop adaptable, flexible students who are capable of anticipating and responding to the changing world of the twenty-first century. This is a significant *leitmotiv* of this chapter. The previous chapter focused on organizing the *content* of the themes, suggesting the need for flexible time management in planning that content. This chapter establishes a set of criteria for planning the delivery of the cross-curricular themes which can be used to evaluate the proposals for styles of delivery from the National Curriculum Council.[1] It is suggested that not only should these proposals be used flexibly but that, beyond this, greater flexibility of teaching and learning styles can be addressed in modular approaches and resource-based flexible learning. These will enable the cross-curricular theses to be taught and learnt more effectively.

Criteria for planning delivery

The previous chapters have argued that the delivery of the cross-curricular themes should ensure that three major factors are addressed:

- the development of *adaptability* (flexibility) in students;
- the development of student *empowerment;*
- the elevation of the *status* of the cross-curricular themes.

Chapter three indicated how these features could be used to evaluate approaches to planning the *content* of the cross-curricular themes. These three features also bear on the planning of teaching and learning styles. The success of a particular teaching and learning style to some extent will lie in its ability to meet these three criteria, and these will be used to evaluate each proposed style. If flexibility in students is a goal of the cross-curricular themes then flexibility of teaching arrangements seems appropriate. If student empowerment is a goal then teaching and learning styles will have to be adopted which foster this, with students learning and practising decision making. If elevation of the status of the themes is a goal then teaching and learning styles which enable students and teachers to accord them high status will be required.

There is a further set of considerations in planning the teaching and learning of the cross-curricular themes. The *Curriculum Guidance* documents state clearly that the cross-curricular themes should be taught and learnt in ways which possess the following characteristics:

- a reliance on practical activities and students' decision making;
- active learning and exploratory activities (open-ended lessons);
- learning by first hand experience and participatory approaches;
- the use of problem-solving approaches;
- the flexible use of a wide range of teaching methods and resources;
- the matching of content with pedagogy;
- the development of collaborative team work – teams of students as well as teams of adults;
- the development of students' abilities to take responsibility for their own learning and their own control of time;
- the development of small-scale projects (in terms of size, numbers of students involved, numbers of adults involved, time allocations) within and outside the school;
- the establishment of links between the school and the wider community outside school, defined widely to include industry, different types of environment, community groups, the infrastructures of communities;
- the development of partnerships between the school and the community.

Though the *Curriculum Guidance* documents accord a place to formal and didactic methods it is quite clear in the documents that the types of experiences being advocated for students should be active and collaborative rather than passive.[2] They should embody several features of student-centred learning (discussed later in this chapter).

This list of features is both reinforced and augmented with reference to the framework for inspection (OFSTED, 1993), where quality of learning and quality of teaching are focuses for inspection. With regard to quality of *learning* OFSTED (1993) details significant indicators of quality: pace; motivation; ability to use skills and understandings; progress; learning skills; attitudes to learning; variety of learning contexts. Several of these lie at the heart of the cross-curricular themes. With regard to quality of *teaching* OFSTED (1993) sets out several indicators of effectiveness: rigour; appropriate teacher expectations; use of relevant strategies; development of skills and understandings; clarity of objectives (of which children are fully aware); subject knowledge; suitable lesson content; activities chosen to promote learning of content; engaging, interesting, motivating and challenging activities; pace; range and fitness for purpose of teaching techniques; positive relationships with children; effectiveness of lesson planning; classroom organization and use of resources; clarity of explanations; quality of questioning; imaginativeness; links between curriculum areas; progression, continuity, relevance, matching, differentiation, balance, richness of provision; regular and positive feedback to children.

The quality of learning and teaching is a function of effective resource management. Here OFSTED (1993) set out three main focuses for their judgements of a school's effectiveness in managing resources:

- *People:* expertise of teaching and non-teaching staff; deployment of specialist and non-specialist teachers; teacher development (INSET and updating which are built into the school development plan); fairness of teaching loads;
- *Resources for learning:* availability, accessibility and equality of access; quantity and quality; efficiency of use; in-school and out-of-school resources (with reference to the quality of liaison with outside bodies, parents, commerce and industry; the use of outsiders to promote learning); relationship of resource provision to the school development plan;
- *Accommodation:* availability; condition; efficiency of use; specialist facilities; accessiblity; quantity and quality; conduciveness to learning.

Clearly the planning of effective delivery of the cross-curricular themes will need to include attention to these important features, which are discussed in subsequent pages of this chapter.

Five modes of delivery from the NCC

The timetabling arrangements in schools will have to be able to embody and develop the approaches set out above. This is a tall order for schools already having to put a quart of content, skills and attitudes development into the pint pot of time available, even working within a slimmer national curriculum. The National Curriculum Council provides some suggestions for how schools might address these features.

It suggests five approaches to timetabling which schools might adopt (cf *Curriculum Guidance 3*):

(i)   permeating the whole curriculum;
(ii)   whole curriculum planning leading to blocks of activities;
(iii) separately timetabled themes;
(iv) taught through separately timetabled PSE;
(v)   long block timetabling.

Each of these approaches is considered below and the advantages and disadvantages of each approach are presented. These approaches need not be mutually exclusive; planners will draw eclectically upon these approaches using the criterion of 'fitness for purpose'.

In many cases the advantages and disadvantages focus on practical difficulties. This is quite deliberate as it indicates that major features of planning for the delivery of the cross-curricular issues are practicability, manageability and feasibility. These are all features of curriculum innovation and change which will be discussed in chapters six and seven.

Permeating the whole curriculum

Though the previous chapter suggested that a permeation approach was a possible means of elevating the status of the cross-curricular themes it can be seen from figure 4.1 that this approach requires planners to address several debatable issues. Figure 4.1 sets out a range of advantages and disadvantages in this approach.

On the one hand this approach is a powerful way of ensuring genuine cross-curricularity, probably the most powerful way of the five outlined by the National Curriculum Council. On the other hand the previous chapter indicated that this approach relies on time-consuming matrix planning to ensure coverage. It requires considerable planning, auditing and co-ordination if it is to be effective. That is very costly of teachers' time. Further, the active, practical nature of learning might be difficult to ensure in subjects where so extended a use of these methods might be seen as inessential and where links with the community outside school might not need to be developed. This is not a method which will reduce timetabled time in schools, even though it might be able to utilise planning by key concepts and key questions to prioritise issues. Although very commendable, this is a high risk strategy as, if it goes wrong, then everyone and all curricula are affected. This needs to be anticipated and planned for at an early stage.

Figure 4.1 − A Permeation Approach

PLANNING BY PERMEATING
THE WHOLE CURRICULUM

Advantages

(i) Secures a place for the themes within the core and foundation; subjects
(ii) responsibility for the themes is shared, building in ownership;
(iii) supports the use of planned block of activities;
(iv) enables themes to be aligned with the most suitable subjects (eg Environmental Education with Geography and Science);
(v) might elevate their status.

Disadvantages

(i) Difficult to monitor appropriate teaching methods;
(ii) may be regarded as a peripheral element within subjects;
(iii) lack of a central focus for each theme can make co-ordination difficult;
(iv) requires a whole school policy for each theme;
(v) may make for inconsistencies of teaching and learning styles;
(vi) the potential for elevating their status may not be realised as they lose their visibility;
(vii) may be difficult to allow sufficient time to explore sensitive and controversial issues;
(viii) may be difficult to co-ordinate themes which lack sharp definition;
(ix) links with subjects might be tenuous;
(x) overall responsibility for the themes might be lost;
(xi) teachers might not possess the subject knowledge of the themes;
(xii) teachers with strong subject loyalties might be resistant to the insertion of what they see as irrelevant content.

Whole curriculum planning leading to blocks of activities

The model of planning indicated in Figure 4.2 has several recommendations. It succeeds in giving a high profile to the cross-curricular themes and possesses the attractions of topic work which were set out in the previous chapter. It possesses considerable potential for integration. Further, it addresses the range of practical experiential

82

Figure 4.2 – Planning for Blocks of Activities

WHOLE CURRICULUM PLANNING LEADING TO BLOCKS OF ACTIVITIES
Advantages
(i) Ensures continuity and progression; (ii) enables decisions to be taken about balance between different curriculum areas; (iii) enables planning for cross-curricular themes to be integrated with other national curriculum subjects; (iv) enables a balance to be achieved between subject specific and integrated methods; (v) it is comparatively straightforward to include cross-curricular themes on the curriculum; (vi) enables a range of experiences, content and skills to be utilised; (vii) makes for relevance to real-life issues; (viii) enables individuals to explore areas of interest to themselves; (ix) enables widespread involvement in and ownership of the cross-curricular themes to be developed – increasing the potential for an elevation of their status; (x) makes co-ordination easier.
Disadvantages
(i) Requires much liaison between staff; (ii) teachers might not have required subject knowledge; (iii) requires a detailed knowledge of programmes for other curriculum areas; (iv) requires whole-school collaborative planning for the short term, medium term and long-term; (v) requires decisions to be taken about how blocks will fit together and how much time will be needed; (vi) requires a whole school policy for each theme which links them to schemes of work for different curriculum areas; (vii) requires an acceptance of differential representation of curriculum areas for different cross-curricular themes; (viii) is very time consuming to plan, audit and assess.

learning situations advocated for the cross-curricular themes (it is no accident that the title of this approach uses the word 'activities'). In doing so it ensures that a very clear set of focuses is established for the activities, enabling large and small scale projects to be developed which can link to the wider community and which develop collaborative team work.

Clearly this approach will require considerable liaison and planning. However it does enable the issue of time management to be addressed and economies of time to be planned through the identification of key experiences. One of the major factors in successful time management – the need to put clear and visible boundaries around time devoted to the themes – is addressed in this form of organization. This approach has very much to recommend it and is one of the major ways in which schools can address cross-curricular issues.

Separately timetabled themes

This approach, set out in Figure 4.3, ensures coverage of the cross-curricular themes. However this is not without its difficulties, principally that genuine cross-curricularity is avoided in this approach and that it exacerbates rather than solves the issue of timetabling. It might be very attractive to schools as it enables theme-specific projects to be developed, a common practice in primary schools.

However, the relationship of these projects to other topic-based approaches is unclear; this approach might separate rather than integrate experiences. What is quite clear is that of all five approaches set out in the *Curriculum Guidance* documents this can accord considerable significance and status to the cross-curricular themes. This is finely balanced, however; it can elevate the status of the themes, alternatively it can marginalise them because this approach separates them from other curricular areas.

Taught through separately timetabled PSE

This approach, set out in Figure 4.4, locates cross-curricular themes in an area of the curriculum with which they are sympathetic – Personal and Social Education.

84

Figure 4.3 – Planning by Separately Timetabled Themes

PLANNING BY SEPARATELY TIMETABLED THEMES

Advantages

(i) Secures a firm and clearly visible place in the curriculum for the cross-curricular themes;
(ii) enhances the possibility for the themes to be taught by specialists;
(iii) possesses considerable potential to elevate the status of the cross-curricular themes;
(iv) facilitates progression and continuity;
(v) ownership of the themes by specialist teachers is strong;
(vi) funding and resourcing is easy to identify and target;
(vii) reduces pressure on large numbers of staff;
(viii) enables high quality delivery of each cross-curricular theme to be addressed more straightforwardly than if the theme is common property of all staff.

Disadvantages

(i) Goes directly against the views that these themes should be *cross*-curricular;
(ii) difficult to find time for these in an already overloaded timetable;
(iii) specific timetabling difficulties in that the nature of the practical activities for the cross-curricular themes might each require large blocks of timetabled time, ie a day or half a day rather than a short period – a particular problem for secondary schools;
(iv) this is a model which can be seen as furthering a subject-based approach – which might fit uncomfortably with many primary school topic-based approaches;
(v) separating them from other national curriculum subjects might marginalise them and lower their status;
(vi) might be very challenging to non-specialists – schools might not be in the position to make new appointments to have the cross-curricular themes taught by specialists;
(vii) puts boundaries round each theme rather than enabling them to be mutually informing.

Figure 4.4 – Parts of a PSE Programme

TAUGHT THROUGH SEPARATELY TIMETABLED PSE
Advantages
(i) Can be taught by a specialist team; (ii) enables strong links to be established between the cross-curricular themes; (iii) the flexibility of a modular structure can be built in, with students learning on specialised programmes; (iv) facilitates progression and continuity; (v) makes considerable room for student contributions; (vi) guarantees that the themes are covered; (vii) ties into an existing timetabling structure; (viii) where PSE programmes are taught by non-specialists it enables many staff to be involved, developing ownership, cross-phase, cross-department and cross-faculty planning to take place; (ix) PSE programmes are easier to modify than other areas of the curriculum; (x) PSE programmes already draw on students' own experiences, ie there is a sympathy in PSE with approaches advocated for delivering cross-curricular themes.
Disadvantages
(i) PSE programmes carry low status in many teachers' and students' eyes, leading to low motivation; (ii) Time available for each cross-curricular theme may be limited; (iii) timetabling for PSE may have to be increased; (iv) may be isolated from other areas of the curriculum; (v) overloads the PSE curriculum; (vi) modular approaches are problematical; (vii) this can be part of a subject-based approach to planning which fits uncomfortably with many primary schools' topic-based approaches; (viii) insufficient timetabled time is available for longer projects of the type advocated in the *Curriculum Guidance* documents;

This enables direct involvement of students' own experiences to be developed and an interrogation of values and beliefs to be undertaken. However, locating them in PSE programmes might be the most problematical aspect of their delivery. It does not reduce timetabled time but adds to it in an area of the curriculum where 'quality' time is often absent, PSE often being viewed by teachers and students as a low status area of the curriculum. Further, locating cross-curricular themes in PSE time is no guarantee that the practical, experiential and project based approaches advocated will be able to be addressed.

A variant of this approach is mentioned in the documents *Health Education* and *Careers Education and Guidance,* where the possibility of locating the cross-curricular themes as parts of a pastoral or tutorial programme is discussed. Several advantages can be claimed for this approach:

- teachers know the students well, which is an important ingredient in discussing values and beliefs:
- nearly all of a school staff will be involved, ie ownership and involvement are shared;
- links are made between pastoral aspects of school and formal school curricula.

However, not only does this approach carry many of the difficulties of locating the cross-curricular themes in PSE programmes, but it carries additional problems:

- many tutorial times are taken up with administrative matters;
- it perpetuates the separation of pastoral programmes and issues from what many teachers see as the 'real business' of teaching – learning academic knowledge;
- teachers may not be specialists in treating sensitive issues;
- this is an approach which is the province of secondary rather than primary schools.

Whereas primary schools tend to deal with pastoral issues both as part of the everyday business of teaching and on an *ad hoc* basis, the tendency has been noted in secondary schools (McGuiness, 1989) of maintaining a distinct line between pastoral and academic issues. McGuiness argues that pastoral care is actually no more nor less than 'good' teaching, ie it should be part of the day-to-day practices of teachers, regardless of the school. This is reinforced by Bowring-Carr (1993) and OFSTED (1993) who include the identification and meeting of students' academic, personal and career needs in their framework for inspection. To place cross-curricular themes into the pastoral and tutorial programme of the school, then, might be to further an undesirable distinction which exists in schools.

Figure 4.5 – Planning by Long Block Timetabling

PLANNING BY LONG-BLOCK TIMETABLING

Advantages

(i) Provides opportunities for activities which cannot be fitted comfortably into normal school timetabling;
(ii) it is congenial to individual resource-based learning and to community-linked activities;
(iii) integrates the cross-curricular themes with the national curriculum subjects;
(iv) intensive and focussed blocks of time can aid student motivation, concentration and memorisation;
(v) it accords high status to the cross-curricular themes, albeit for only a short time, by making them visible and the main focuses of study;
(vi) enables continuity and progression to be planned;
(vii) ensures coverage of the cross-curricular themes;
(viii) links with the community can be strengthened;
(ix) can enable small teams of staff to plan projects, ie it develops ownership and makes for manageability.

Disadvantages

(i) It can marginalise the cross-curricular themes as short-lived but 'special' and discontinuous activities;
(ii) requires considerable planning by a team;
(iii) it might require teaching and learning methods which make new demands on teachers and students;
(iv) placing great emphasis on activities which focus on the cross-curriculum theme(s) might render links with other national curriculum areas minimal, ie the unrelatedness to other subjects might diminish their cross-curricular potential;
(v) might be insufficent for handling all aspects of the cross-curricular themes;
(vi) might make heavy demands on resources;
(vii) accords disproportionate significance to student absence.

Long block timetabling

What is emerging so far is a picture of the cross-curricular themes which suggests that by confining them regularly to short blocks of timetabled time risks losing the experiential, community-focused and project-based aspects of the themes. Long block timetabling avoids these difficulties. The advantages and disadvantages of long block timetabling are set out in Figure 4.5.

Here schools might adopt a 'sixth day' timetable or introduce specific 'activity' weeks to cover the cross-curricular themes. This method of delivering the cross-curricular themes has very many attractions as it enables the practical, experiential aspects of the themes to be addressed fully. Freeing large blocks of time enables community-focused projects to be developed in a fully-fledged way (eg the example of a project on 'shops' for primary children in the document *Education for Economic and Industrial Understanding* and work placements in secondary schools). This provides room in the school calendar for those cross-curricular activities which require extended time frames. It is a method of delivery which can do full justice to the criteria for effective delivery set out at the beginning of this chapter. Further, though it implies that one or more weeks of a school year will be taken up with the cross-curricular themes, this might be a more productive – and hence more economical – use of time than allocating specific sessions each week to the themes.

A 'sixth day' timetabling arrangement signals a fundamental shift of planning which is crucial for addressing the *flexibility* of teaching arrangements which, this chapter suggests, is an essential component of the content and delivery of the cross-curricular themes. This approach recognizes that the school timetable in fact is mutable and can accommodate flexible demands rather than being cast in tablets of stone to be delivered rigidly every week regardless of how fitting this is for the subject matter being treated. This is a factor which has long been recognised by teachers of Art and Music, where confining activities to hour-long blocks is inappropriate. After all, a painting cannot always be fitted conveniently into an hour long block. Primary schools have long recognised this feature and allowed for it in blocking out times of the week for project work. In this approach timing varies according to the demands of the tasks and the ways in which children are progressing through them.

Modular organisation of the modes of delivery

It was suggested earlier that the need for developing adaptable and responsible students should have its parallel in the development of flexible organizations of delivery. This has been the practice in primary schools for many years, by dint of the tradition of having largely one teacher to one class, ie where the organization of curricula, a group of children and time is under the control of a single person. In secondary schools the rise of modular approaches offers a significant step forward in matching flexibility of curriculum organization with the development of autonomy in students through the notion of responsible, counselled action planning.

A modular approach is simply an organizational device (Moon, 1988) (with respect to students, curricula and time) which can be used to deliver the cross-curricular themes in any or all of the five modes of delivery outlined above. Casting the five modes of delivery set out by the National Curriculum Council into modular approaches and organizations has several attractions over more traditional forms of organization:

- each module has short-term achievable goals which are recognisable by students, ie it can improve student motivation (an indicator of quality which is recognised by OFSTED (1993);
- each module has high internal coherence which is clear to the students;
- self-contained modules can become part of a greater whole (ie a within-module and between-module view of progression and continuity can be adopted);
- modules can be subject-specific to single or to several cross-curricular themes, a combination of subjects and themes, cross-subject, cross-department, cross-faculty, cross-phase;
- modules are useful ways of addressing key concepts, each key concept or set of key concepts becoming the organizing principle of the module;
- assessment takes place at the end of modules rather than at the end of a series of courses, ie feedback and certification are almost immediate and students can demonstrate what they have learnt (a useful way of providing assessment evidence);
- modules fit comfortably into objectives-based planning, action planning, unit accreditation (in secondary schools) and a Record of Achievement;
- modules can be useful in managing scarce resources;
- modules enable one or more year groups to be taught together;
- modules enable students to experience contrasting types of module during a term or named period of time;
- modules make for teamwork amongst staff;

- modules can promote student autonomy and responsibility through enabling choices of modules to be planned, particularly if several modules are to be made available over a two-year period.

These attractions are very considerable as they concern curriculum content, organisation and choice, staffing structures and team approaches. It will be argued in chapters six and seven that these are vital for the planning and implementation of the cross-curricular themes. Further, a modular approach addresses resource allocation, student autonomy and decision making, and flexible timetabling. In modular approaches, then, several of the major issues in and criteria for delivering the cross-curricular themes outlined at the start of this chapter are addressed.

On the other hand there are anxieties about modular approaches to organising learning. These indicate that a modular approach is more than simply an organizational device but impacts on views of knowledge, interpersonal relationships and learning. The main worries can be summed up thus:

- modules can be short-term and behavioural, leading to a trivialisation of the curriculum;
- there is a risk that developing relationships between students and tutors will be threatened as they will only meet each other for short blocks of time;
- modules can be time-consuming to develop;
- it can be laborious to fit the assessments of cross-subject, cross-theme, cross-subject and theme, cross-faculty modules within national frameworks of assessment which are subject-specific (a particular problem for GCSE examinations where examination boards tend to be subject-specific);
- counselling of students will have to address the issue of fragmentation of learning, ie procedures and rationales for option choices will have to be clarified; the greater the number of modules there are, the greater will be the need and time for counselling on module choice;
- modules may need to carry different weightings if progression is to be addressed;
- compatibility and comparability of modules might be difficult to establish;
- modules are frequently organised in terms of curriculum content, thereby neglecting attention to individual differences and needs in students, ie the uniformity of a module might serve *curriculum* differentiation well but *student-centred* differentiation less well;

- failure on one module might well result in failure of a whole course (ie a disproportionate emphasis is placed on passing each module);
- the need for clarification of pathways, core and optional modules has to be addressed;
- in the interests of organisational ease there is a risk of uniformity of time scales for modules (eg 30 hours of teaching) which might be inappropriate for some aspects of learning.

With regard to the five modes of delivery a modular organisation can embrace a *permeation* approach. As modules frequently combine several areas of the core and foundation subjects of the national curriculum (ie where they already permeate each other) there is no reason why the cross-curricular themes cannot be included in these combinations. Exactly the same process can occur in planning the whole curriculum in terms of *blocks of activities.* One or more cross-curricular themes themselves can be modularised so that they can be delivered by *separately timetabled themes,* either singly or in combination, though generally this approach was not recommended in the earlier discussion. Just as separately timetabled PSE is frequently modularised (eg into modules on health, relationships and self-awareness) the cross-curricular themes can be an element of a modular PSE programme. Finally, *long block timetabling* enables the cross-curricular themes to fit comfortably into a modular approach where a module can take place over a week's activitites, a week long project, an 'environmental week' or suchlike. A modular approach is very compatible with the five modes of delivery of the cross-curricular themes suggested by the National Curriculum Council. Moreover, if attention is paid to varying lengths of modules, student choice of modules and the development of interdisciplinary modules, this approach to curriculum organization meets very fully the criteria for successful development of the cross-curricular themes set out at the start of this chapter.

Modular approaches, then, can be used to organise the delivery of the cross-curricular themes in terms of the five approaches from the National Curriculum Council. However planners will have to consider the effects which portioning curricula into smaller units (modules) exert on *students, knowledge, teachers, curricula* and *assessment.*

For example modular approaches could lead to students regarding *knowledge* and learning as the aggregation of isolated, discrete pieces of information. Teachers may regard the considerable time involved in developing modules as time badly spent because it detracts from the need for subject specific knowledge to be taught in order to pass examinations. Further, they may regard the potential loss of developing knowledge of students as detrimental to being able to plan for their specific needs. With regard to *curricula,* there is a danger that *within-module* progression might take precedence over *between-module* progression. With regard to *assessment,* modular curricula might neglect the long-term aspects of education and the overall, unmeasurable development of students because emphasis has been laid on the demonstration of short term behaviours. Here the backwash effect of modular structures onto curricula could result in a narrowing of curricula to cover that which can be assessed straightforwardly at the end of a module.

Modular approaches have their place but that place is not exclusive; teachers will have to decide which aspects of the cross-curricular themes will be best approached through a modular structure and how far a modular structure will be able to deliver the cross-curricular themes to the full. The criterion of 'fitness for purpose' is the touchstone in deciding how modular approaches can take their place alongside other approaches to delivering the cross-curricular themes.

Implementing the five modes of delivery

If flexibility is to be built into the timetabling then this will recognise that, in fact, schools will not be able simply to opt in to one specific model of delivery but, rather, that all of these modes of delivery can be utilised together. This is a major and unavoidable feature of curriculum planning for the cross-curricular themes, just as it is for other aspects of the curriculum. It will require planners to identify:

- which elements of the cross-curricular themes are best addressed through, or require, a permeation approach;
- which elements of the cross-curricular themes are best approached through, or require, whole curriculum planning leading to blocks of activities;
- which elements of the cross-curricular themes are best approached through, or require, separate timetabling of the themes;
- which elements of the cross-curricular themes are best approached through, or require, making the themes part of a PSE programme or part of a pastoral and tutorial programme;
- which elements of the cross-curricular themes are best approached through, or require, long block timetabling;
- which elements of the cross-curricular themes can fit comfortably into shorter blocks of time and which require longer blocks of time;
- which elements of the cross-curricular themes require resources

external to the school and which can be managed within the school's resources;

- which elements of the cross-curricular themes require specialist knowledge and which do not;
- which elements of the cross-curricular themes require many staff and which do not;
- which elements of the cross-curricular themes are heavy on resources (however defined) and which are not.

This is a large undertaking, but, as with most curriculum innovations, this is an unavoidable requisite for success. It will be suggested in chapters six and seven that this might best be undertaken by a development team or teams.

The approaches outlined so far have considered the issue of time as a resource. However the notion of resources is wider than this. If flexibility is to be developed further, and if the criterion of developing in students responsibility for their own learning and control of time is to be addressed fully then the notion of flexibility will need to be expanded to include flexibility of resources in a wide sense, for example:

- human resources (eg teachers, students, community representatives);
- material resources;
- resources of time;
- resources of space;
- administrative support structures;
- expertise – within and outside the school;
- the nature and size of groupings of students (including individual work, pairs, groups with up to four or five members, classes of thiry students, 'doubled-up' or 'trebled-up' classes of up to one hundred students);
- specialist resources.

An example of the notion of time as a resource which must feature in the rationale of curriculum planning can be seen in the notion of team teaching. Here introductory sessions taken by a single teacher with a large number of students might free preparation time for other teachers. Putting together several groups of students or having groups constituted, dissolved and reconstituted on a variety of criteria recognises that flexibility of time is, in fact, a function of flexibility of resources. It is in this field that Knight's (1991) work on timetabling has much to offer (discussed in the previous chapter). He indicates how close attention to the nature, flexibility, quantity, quality, structure and organisation of time during the day, term and year will enable planners to identify where time might be managed more effectively to promote learning. A close analysis of time will enable its use to be rationalised.

Resource-based flexible learning

As an extension to the flexibility of time and delivery suggested by the five modes of delivery and modular approaches outlined above, planners may find it useful to turn to developments in resource-based flexible learning (Eraut *et al,* 1991). This approach can be regarded as the most flexible of all the approaches suggested so far. It can be seen, therefore, as that approach which most fully addresses the criteria for effective delivery of the cross-curricular themes outlined at the start of this chapter.

The early part of this book indicated that preparing students, teachers and curricula to cope with change is a pressing priority in education. Since the early 1980s the rise of information technology in schools has revolutionised data access, storage and retrieval. A new mentality has to come into schools to accommodate this. It is not necessarily enough to continue to organise schools in existing frames of teaching and learning styles, deployment and use of staff, timetabling arrangements, resourcing and resource use. This is to try to meet new demands with old practices. The instrument which addresses all of these concerns and suggests a way forward is that of 'resource-based flexible learning'.

This notion builds on the increased flexibility of resource use (where resources are defined widely – see earlier) and aims to give the student increased responsibility for the organisation and content of her own learning – individually or in groups – accompanied by appropriate teacher support. It sits very comfortably with the cross-curricular themes as it addresses key elements in the themes:

- positive and adaptable learning environments;
- the development of needs-driven programmes of study;
- developed relations with individuals and groups outside school;
- the use of up-to-date resources;
- the use of target-setting and action planning to negotiate individual profiles of learning, recorded in a Record of Achievement;
- an ability to recast teacher and learner relationships where teachers are facilitators, advisers, joint reviewers, joint planners and tutors. Teachers are non-threatening, non-authoritarian, negotiating tasks and activities and building and working on contracts with students (formally and informally), thereby welding pastoral concerns with learning concerns;

- an ability to accommodate changes in curriculum content and skills whilst still preserving (and indeed furthering) important characteristics of the curriculum: breadth, balance, continuity and progression, relevance, differentiation;
- an ability to use flexibly resources of *time, spaces* purpose-built spaces, eg laboratories, libraries and non-purpose-built spaces, in-school and out-of-school resources), *people* (other students, teachers, technicians, parents, community representatives, local commerce and industry resources, librarians), *materials* and reprographics, *organisation of curricula* (eg modular approaches – both short and long modules);
- an active, experiential approach to learning;
- flexible and mutable groupings of students as dictated by purposes, eg exploratory work, role play, discussion groups, support groups, task-oriented groups, peer tutoring, practical tasks, problem-solving approaches, surveys, case studies;
- use of information technology, community resource use;
- an ability to accommodate new assessment arrangements, including formal assessment requirements, teacher and student self-assessment and subsequent target-setting (an *ipsative* process), records of achievement (which are strong on 'ownership'), criterion-referencing, diagnostic, open recording.

Clearly schools will have to build up to this style of teaching and learning as it is contingent on three main features:

(i) students' abilities to handle this form of teaching and learning;
(ii) staffs' abilities to handle this form of teaching and learning;
(iii) sufficient appropriate resources (defined widely to include materials, people, time, space, administrative support). Having only a few packages of material resources will reduce rather than further flexibility.

With regard to *students* the student-centred approach can begin from the early days of a child's entry into school (eg using the High Scope project (Hohmann *et al,* 1979). It can continue through primary and secondary education. Even though much of the documentation about flexible learning has focused on students of 14 years and older, eg in documentation of TVEI and its successors, this does not confine it to the secondary sphere only; indeed flexible learning systems have been operating in primary schools for years, albeit without this title. This approach involves developing students' abilities to manage a variety of factors as set out in Figure 4.6 below, eg time; relationships; planning, implementation and evaluation of their own work; data accessing; learning styles. All of these are indicators of quality in learning which feature in a school inspection (OFSTED, 1993). In short this means the development of empowerment in students – their ability to handle increasing freedoms. Further, giving greater control of learning to students can be a potent way of raising their motivation. Raising student motivation is a significant way of raising the status of the cross-curricular themes.

The planned move to flexible learning will have to take account of personalities and responsibilities in students. A gradualist approach to implementing flexible learning can be adopted, increasing:

- the curriculum coverage;
- the time slots used;
- the amount of time blocked for flexible learning;
- the number of teachers involved;
- the range of resources used.

This will enable students to develop the skills required to work effectively in such an approach and will enable teachers to identify students' needs and stage the introduction and implementation of this style of learning.

With regard to *teachers* the move to flexible learning constitutes a major change in teaching styles. Several staff may need to be persuaded of the relative advantage of this style over existing styles as some teachers will have to change their attitudes, values, practices, organisation and relationships with other teachers and students. Chapters six and seven discuss the significance of this and how it might be approached. The move to introducing flexible learning may well require staff to be released from some timetabled responsibilities in order to develop these elements.

The implications for students and teachers of the moves to student-centred flexible learning are summarised in Figure 4.6.

With regard to *resources* one can envisage an 'open-learning' or 'flexible learning' suite in which are housed an array of resources: books, library and resource materials, computers, reprographic facilities, audio- and video-cassette facilities, on-line and off-line information accessing facilities, bays where teachers could discuss work with students, working bays and carrels – large and small, wet and dry areas. Clearly this might be suitable for certain areas of the curriculum only. Where specialist facilities are required or maybe where expensive equipment or materials are being used then necessary support services and specialist rooms will have to be provided. Students will need to be

Figure 4.6 – Implications of Flexible Learning

IMPLICATIONS OF FLEXIBLE LEARNING

For Students

(i) Managing their own time;
(ii) Managing relationships with other students and teachers (eg non-authoritarian relationships with adults);
(iii) Planning, implementing and evaluating their own work;
(iv) Accessing information from a variety of sources and in a variety of forms;
(v) Working individually and collaboratively.

For Teachers

(i) Group approaches to planning and working;
(ii) Developing abilities in tutoring and discussion;
(iii) Designing and collecting new materials;
(iv) Building on differing staff expertise;
(v) Dissemination of effective practice;
(vi) Organisation of curricula and resources;
(vii) Corporate goal setting;
(viii) Monitoring and evaluation;
(ix) Piloting;
(x) Openness and dialogue;
(xi) A recognition that teachers are also learners;
(xii) Supportive management structures.

able to access, use and replace openly available resources and those where supervision is required.

There are several resource implications of this approach. Consideration will have to be given to the planning and organisation of space so that the location of and access to centralised and de-centralised resources is clear and rational. This begs the major question of building up resources at a time when financial constraints are very severe in schools, even though LMS might enable funds to be targeted to specific innovations. The development of resource-based, student-centred flexible learning, however, need not be an all-or-nothing approach, it can be developed piecemeal. Further this approach marks a move away from 'sets' of books or materials to providing less copies but a wider range of books and other materials.

One of the major resource concerns of this approach is its use of the teacher as a resource. Traditionally the one-teacher-to-one class approach was seen to be highly economical in terms of teacher time and in terms of using the teacher's knowledge and expertise. These need not be a casualty of flexible-learning approaches. Indeed, given the need to preserve a vital ingredient of education – developing relationships between students and adults – it is essential that students do not learn simply by proxy – using worksheets and non-human resources to replace the teacher. Flexible learning will still have the facility for group and whole class sessions. The use of the teacher as a knowledge and pedagogical resource continues to be vital and central. The experience of primary schools is an example of this, where a flexible learning approach has often characterised the nature of topic work. Here the teacher punctuates individual and group activity by formal input to the whole class or smaller groups, whole-class preparation, discussions, feedback and review. One of the pedagogical principles which primary school teachers have known for years is that too devolved an approach results in the teacher simply repeating points several times to different groups (or even to the same group!). That is an abuse of flexible learning and is inefficient use of teacher expertise.

Hence what is being argued in flexible learning systems is the ability of these to extend rather that to replace existing teaching arrangements. They augment the range of teaching and learning styles, thereby meeting several of the criteria for quality teaching and learning set out by OFSTED (1993) and referred to at the start of this chapter. This enables managed flexibility to be developed which is apposite to the cross-curricular themes rather than representing an adherence to a single philosophy of introducing so much flexibility that 'anything goes'.

Flexible learning, then, is a powerful and highly appropriate though not exclusive means of meeting the demands of the cross-curricular themes. Though it requires careful and organised resourcing its ultimate success also depends upon people as well as materials.

Summary

This chapter has argued that if the timetabling and pedagogical requirements of the cross-curricular themes are to be addressed then more than one single approach is needed. In order to meet the cross-curricular aims of developing adaptable students who can show a measure of initiative, autonomy and responsibility in working individually or in groups a flexible approach to delivery is required. The strengths and weaknesses of each of the five modes of delivery outlined in the *Curriculum Guidance* documents were discussed. It was argued that these were useful if taken together rather than opting for a single mode of delivery. It was suggested that modular approaches to curriculum planning could embody all five modes of delivery of the cross-curricular themes and meet the demands of flexibility in planning the cross-curricular themes. Further, modular approaches were seen to address very effectively the criteria for delivery set out at the start of this chapter and to develop flexible and empowered students. Some important strengths and weaknesses of modular approaches were outlined and it was suggested that a combination of modular and alternative approaches would be necessary if the complexity of the cross-curricular themes were to be captured.

It was argued that these approaches could be extended through a shift of vision to embrace the developing field of resource-driven flexible learning. In this, it was argued, lay the potential to meet most fully the flexibility of the cross-curricular themes and the flexibility and adaptability required for next century's citizens. However the success of this approach was seen to be contingent upon students, teachers and resources. The potential for motivating students in this approach was seen to be an important feature in according status to the cross-curricular themes. It was argued that this approach could be developed gradually in a way which would allow students and teachers to familiarise themselves with its rationales and operation and would enable resources to be developed over time, a feature which recognised the financial constraints upon schools. In suggesting that there was a risk in this approach of losing sight of a central pillar of education – the development of relationships and the use of teachers as a resource – it was argued that flexible learning should take its place alongside the other modes of delivery outlined in this chapter. Teachers continue to be centrally important in student-centred flexible learning.

In deciding which parts of the cross-curricular themes should be delivered by each of the various modes either separately or in combination the argument suggested that the criterion of 'fitness for purpose' should be the guiding principle.

Notes

1. This chapter uses the term 'delivery' as it is in common parlance. However, one should not overlook the mechanistic overtones of this metaphor which oversimplify the processes of teaching and learning and the professionalism of the teacher. An interesting exposé of this can be seen in Bowring-Carr (1993).

2. This is a view which is firmly rooted in a theory of learning from Vygotsky which stresses that higher cognitive processes have social origins, indeed that these are socially transmitted (Jausovec, 1990).

CHAPTER FIVE

Assessment and the Cross-Curricular Themes

Introduction

Assessment is a process of gathering information on the quality of a student's performance in named fields and making a judgement about the student's performance in the light of that information. It involves measuring, grading or commenting on a student's performance in the light of criteria, either comparing students with each other (norm-referencing) or individually with a specific set of standards or criteria (criterion-referencing).

This chapter sets out a range of issues which assessors will have to address if reliable and useful results are to be gathered. The chapter proceeds in four stages: *firstly* it sets assessment in context, arguing that planners have to be aware of the several uses to which assessments can be put. *Secondly* it identifies a range of factors which stem from these contexts, arguing that considerable caution has to be exercised in developing and using assessments. *Thirdly* it deals with instruments to gather data, arguing that 'fitness for purpose' must be tempered by practicality and indicating how this tension might be addressed. *Finally* it addresses the reporting and recording of assessments.

The contexts of assessment

One can set assessment in several contexts: accountability, education and the economy, political demands, educational improvement, and the development of new assessment instruments and practices.

Firstly, with regard to making schools and teachers *accountable,* the increase in assessment activity is indicative of a rising managerialism in education which has its outcomes in several issues: appraisal; the increased bureaucratisation of education; performance-related pay; line-management models of staff organisation; the introduction of conditions for teachers' pay and working practices; the opening up of schools to public scrutiny.

Secondly, the links between *education and the economy* have witnessed the resurfacing of the debate about the role that education should play in preparing students for working life. In terms of the cross-curricular themes this is evidenced in the documents *Education for Economic and Industrial Understanding, Careers Education and Guidance* and *Education for Citizenship.* It is no accident, perhaps, that these three themes are very fully explicated in the *Curriculum Guidance* documents and that the theme of *Education for Economic Understanding* has received the most number of supplementary guideline documents.

Thirdly, in terms of the *political* context of education we are witness to an increased centralism and *dirigiste* control of both the content and the assessment of the curriculum.[1] This is evidenced in the conflation of the National Curriculum Council and the Schools Examination and Assessment Authority into the School Curriculum and Assessment Authority, tying together curricula and assessment.

Fourthly, in terms of *educational improvement* it was made explicit that the national curriculum, backed by clear assessments, would improve standards (DES, 1987). This can be taken further with the introduction of school management plans and the increase in inspection activity. Indeed OFSTED (1993) includes in its inspections a comparison between a school's and national norms of student achievement together with a requirement that standards be as high as possible. The notion of educational improvement through increased assessment commits the 'measurement fallacy' − that the more one measures an item the greater that item will become (the 'weighing a pig' mentality − the more one weighs the pig the larger it will grow, regardless of feeding or inputs of resources!).

Finally, with regard to the *development of new assessment instruments and practices,* the use of Records of Achievement and the National Record of Achievement (NRA) signals a move towards assessing and recording a wide range of curricular and extra-curricular achievements which are criterion-related.

What is very clear is that assessment of the cross-curricular themes serves a variety of purposes. Simply to accept that the cross-curricular themes should be included in the assessments of the student's achievement of the national curriculum is to beg an immense question. Whilst the formal assessment of students' achievements in the cross-curricular themes might be a way of enhancing the status of the themes, there is a very powerful case to be made against the suggestion that the cross-curricular themes should be assessed at all. Including the cross-curricular themes in formal assessment is to play out an agenda of increasing assessment of every aspect of a student's development. It can mark the further encroachment on an individual's privacy, particularly if attitudes and personality factors are to be included.

Because the themes concern unmeasurable experiences (discussed below) one can argue that these should remain students' private property in large part or should be reported in the students' own terms. To record achievement in the cross-curricular themes might be to destroy the very specific excitement, meaning and creativity which inheres in them. Teachers will have to ask themselves why they wish to assess a non-statutory element of the curriculum. Students should realise that curriculum elements can be important even if they are not assessed.

If assessment of students' achievements of the cross-curricular themes is to take place then teachers will have to ask what should and should not be assessed in the themes. Assessment is as much a moral issue as is the selection of curricula.

The purposes of assessment

The purposes of assessment within the context of the national curriculum were spelt out in the TGAT report (DES, 1988b) as being:

- formative (diagnostic);
- criterion-referenced;
- moderated;
- related to progression.

The great strength of the increased emphasis on the need for assessment *evidence* since the TGAT report has several beneficial aspects:

- it relies on fact rather than teachers' hunches or prejudices;
- it can improve the level of match between children and curricula;
- it can further diagnostic teaching;
- it should ensure a wide curriculum diet if reliability and validity are to be addressed;
- it requires a variety of teaching and learning styles to be adopted.

In short, assessment can improve the quality of programming, pedagogy and diagnosis in scope and depth.

On the other hand one can detect concerns and problems within TGAT's four purposes. With regard to the *formative* and *diagnostic* purposes of assessment the Task Group on Assessment and Testing argued that once a detailed diagnosis of students' abilities has been made this would shape the programmes of work and experiences to be prepared for students. This might require extensive record-keeping and recording of the planning which has taken place. Clearly this is time consuming and will have to be tempered by practicality and utility. Furthermore there is a certain danger in using diagnostic and formative date summatively as indicators of the performance of schools and teachers. Here data acquired for one set of purposes – diagnosis, forward planning, evaluation of programme effectiveness – might be used for a different set of purposes – measuring school and teacher quality and using data for the purposes of accountability. The issue here concerns the ethics of using assessment data. Further, the backwash effect of using assessment might lead teachers to teach narrowly to aspects of the national curriculum. This might be a constraining rather than liberating course of action which devalues that which is not assessed.

With regard to *criterion-referencing* this has given renewed impetus to the behavioural objectives movement and competency testing. Here every behaviour is planned for, every outcome is predetermined and students and teachers become passive recipients of curricula. Managing this has given rise to the development of 'tick-sheets' of behaviours and testing rather than assessing in a variety of forms. This has also led to a falsely dichotomous view of success – where the child either can or cannot perform a specific behaviour, where the child either has or has not achieved a particular objective or level of attainment.

With regard to *moderation* the expense of this exercise is vast in terms of time yet the task of ensuring inter-rater reliability is necessary if it is to be worthwhile, legitimate and credible.

If *progression* is to be linked to differentiation the outcome could assume a unidirectional view of learning through the levels. This overlooks the fact that, as many teachers know, children's learning is eclectic and recursive. Moreover, if progression is to be linked to differentiation the outcome could easily lead to reliance on expensive individualised schemes. This moves away from the collaborative nature of learning the cross-curricular themes which is advocated by the National Curriculum Council.

In addition to the concerns about interpreting TGAT's four purposes of assessment one can detail a list of concerns which spring from the development of assessment in the national curriculum. These can be set out thus:

- *technical details:* there does not appear to be parity between the levels of demand for different cross-curricular themes. It is questionable whether the key stage tasks actually correspond to hierarchies of difficulty as students of different ages make qualitatively different responses to the same task, ie maturation of students is important but overlooked in national assessments. Higher levels might not subsume lower levels of attainment, ie a pupil might be able to perform a level three task but not a level two task (Whetton, Ruddock and Hopkins, 1991; Wiliam, 1993). Further, the number of contexts in which behaviours must be observed for a judgement to be made of whether the student has achieved a particular level of attainment has not been clarified. This might lead to infinite assessment if reliability is to be addressed. Behaviours observed in one context might not generalise to another, ie one generalises at one's peril. The form of assessments needs to address the significance of equal opportunities (for example, where girls perform better than boys in continuous assessment, where boys do better than girls in multiple choice items (DES, 1988b)).
- *aggregating assessment results:* the requirement that assessment results should be aggregated into whole subjects (or, in this context, whole themes) loses the purpose of criterion-referencing (that the assessments should be very specific and diagnostic).
- *contextual factors:* context exerts a strong effect on performance. The way in which the task is presented to the student can exert a large effect on the student's performance. Nerves and the Hawthorne effect[2] can lower the reliability of the results. The particular operation which is to be assessed can be blotted out by the size and the complexity of related factors (eg language used, readability, size of numbers in an algorithm). The number, stages and types of operation required can be overwhelming even though children might be able to tackle each component element.

This catalogue of worries can be minimised in assessing students' achievements of the cross-curricular themes if a greater emphasis is placed on teacher and student-led assessments. Such assessments can be diagnostic and formative, ie feeding into action planning. If teachers build on the knowledge that they have of students and their performances in given contexts then reliability can be increased. Teachers can adopt a selective approach in deciding what to assess and what to report. This enables criterion referencing to be addressed and moves away from a 'tick sheet' mentality and enhances the worthwhileness of assessments. Moderation is enhanced through having a team approach to planning, delivery and assessment (discussed in chapter seven). Progression is defined ipsatively, ie in the students' own terms. This is a far more flexible view of progression than the linear model of the national curriculum and yet, as assessment is a shared matter, this does not mean that students will not be 'stretched'. In short, what is being required in assessments is utility, reliability, validity and worthwhileness of assessments. These can be addressed in a streamlined, selective, open-ended assessment which builds on teachers' professional assessments and students' self assessments.

Devising assessments of cross-curricular themes

Assessments must actually be workable. It is fruitless to plan assessments of baroque splendour if they cannot be undertaken in everyday teaching. This section sets out a range of factors which will have to be addressed in planning assessments if the concerns voiced earlier are to be minimised and practicality is to be addressed. It indicates how these can be applied to the cross-curricular themes. Ten factors are set out here. For each factor a series of words, phrases and questions is presented in order to clarify issues within each factor.

Factor One: decide what to assess – the *focus* of the assessment.

Points to consider: the scope of the assessment (eg covering one cross-curricular theme or several themes; one element of the theme or several; one key concept or several key concepts – within one cross-curricular theme or across several). Given that the cross-curricular themes might be taught singly or in combination with other themes and national curriculum subjects, it is necessary to identify appropriate assessment evidence. Special problems occur during field work in the cross-curricular themes where intangible development might result from out-of-school links or where performance is only able to be captured in a fleeting instance (akin to the problem of assessment in music or in physical education where the assessment has to be on-the-spot);

Factor Two: decide how to incorporate assessment into the daily activities of children and teaching – the *context* of the assessment.

Points to consider: ensure that there is minimal disruption to the ways of working with the cross-curricular themes; consider the group formations and dynamics; keep to existing timetabling and staffing arrangements; keep to existing teaching and learning styles (ie avoid 'engineering' a task); clarify where the assessment of the cross-curricular themes will take place — in school, out of school — so that it is not an out-of-the-ordinary routine but integral to teaching and learning.

If 'normality' is to be maintained in assessing cross-curricular themes then this might require an emphasis on observational data and *post hoc* reporting rather than on purpose-made tests. This is particularly true if the assessment necessarily has to take place out of the school. Where a collaborative activity or enterprise for a cross-curricular project or theme is undertaken by a small or large group it may not be possible or desirable to parcel out each student's contribution to the collective enterprise, hence a group assessment might be appropriate.

Factor Three: decide when and how often to assess and record, how long the assessment activity will last — the *timing* of the assessment.

Points to consider: the time of the day, week, term, year to assess; how to avoid setting more assessment tasks for fast workers; how to avoid setting repeated assessment activities for slower workers (ie how to avoid generating a sense of failure); what time constraints to set on the assessment activity. The timing of the assessment will have to link to the timetabling arrangements of the cross-curricular themes — permeation, PSE session, long block timetabling etc. as mentioned in chapter four — so that fidelity to the existing arrangements is assured.

Factor Four: decide what kinds of information are required to yield valid evidence of achievement — the *validity* of the assessment.

Points to consider: how will the assessments address construct validity (ie determining the extent to which the assessments address the psychological constructs involved in a programme, eg creativity, imagination, engagement, enterprise)? How will the assessments address content validity (ie determining whether the assessments address in sufficient depth and breadth the items that they are supposed to be assessing)? How will the assessments addresss concurrent validity (ie the extent to which the results of the assessments of given elements would concur with results from other means of assessing the same elements)? Evidence of knowledge, concepts, skills, attitudes, learning styles, methods of enquiry, methods of self-evaluation might feature in the assessment information. However a selective approach will mean that decisions will have to be taken about the level of specificity of the assessment in order to avoid unnecessary detail and reportage.

Factor Five: decide appropriate tasks and activities — the *validity* and *match* of the tasks.

108

Points to consider: how will the task be introduced – the *presentation mode* (DES, 1988b) – (eg orally, written etc.)? How will students work in the activity – the *operation mode* (ibid.) – (eg, written, oral, practical)? How will students demonstrate the outcome of the task – the *response mode* – eg answering a multiple-choice test, written, oral, practical demonstration, a product? Are all of the tasks which are required equally difficult? If not then what is it that makes some tasks easier or more difficult than others? How will tasks be selected? How many tasks are necessary for a student to complete successfully before being credited with having reached the required standard? How related to everyday student life are the tasks? What are the task demands for each student? Is the task a repeat of an activity undertaken previously? Is it a task which requires students to apply existing knowledge in a new situation or context? Is it a task which is organised for the students or which they will have to organise for themselves? How will the gathering of evidence of differential demands in a group activity be planned and implemented?

Factor six: decide how the evidence will be acquired – the *methods* or *instruments.*

Points to consider: what methods are most suitable for the nature, content and pedagogy of the cross-curricular themes? Under what circumstances will various methods be used, for example *observation* (visual and aural), – structured, semi-structured, unstructured (incidental and unplanned), *interviews* – structured, semi-structured, open-ended (ie incidental, unplanned and conversational), *records and notes* kept by the teacher, *diaries* kept by the student, *videotape, audiotape, photograph, testing, documentary evidence* – formal and informal written accounts or other forms of documentation?

Factor Seven: decide how to build out distorting influences on students' performances and behaviours – the *validity* and *reliability* of the assessment.

Points to consider: how well motivated is the student? How threatening or unthreatening are the conditions in which the assessment will take place? How positive are the relationships between the assessors and the students? How will blocks to reliability be minimised (eg readability, 'nerves', the size and complexity of the task, the number of sub-tasks required in the overall task, the familiarity of the student with the way of working required)? How will consistency between different assessors (inter-rater reliability) be assured?[3] How relevant and important will the student consider the task to be? How should outsiders be involved in assessment (and how will parity of assessments by different outsiders with different agendas be assured?[4]

Factor Eight: decide how to interpret the data and information yielded by the assessment – the clarification of the *criteria* for assessment.

Points to consider: how much should the students be made aware of assessment criteria before the activity or task? From where do these criteria come? How are the criteria prioritised and translated into practice? Are all of the elements of the cross-curricular themes operationalisable (able to be translated in practice)? How will non-operational elements be assessed? Are there 'degrees of citizenship' or of 'economic understanding'?

Factor Nine: decide how to build ongoing records into a less frequent formal record – the *sampling* and *selection* of assessment data.

Points to consider: how frequently will the record be updated? How can representative achievements of the student be recorded? How will every cross-curriculum theme be sampled? Should the evidence be of the same types within and across all of the cross-curricular themes? Should non-statutory elements of the national curriculum (the cross-curricular themes) be reported as part of a formal, statutory document of record? Should non-statutory elements of the national curriculum be assessed and recorded in the same way as the statutory elements of the national curriculum?

Factor Ten: decide how to present the results of the assessment – the issues of *reporting*.

Points to consider: who are the audiences of the report? Will the report need to be modified to suit different audiences? How will data be summarised? How will the aggregation of data preserve criterion referencing? Should records of students' achievements in the cross-curricular themes be made public? Should the assessment results of the cross-curricular themes only appear as positive statements in a Record of Achievement?

These ten factors not only enable effective assessment to be planned but also feature as key criteria in the inspection of a school's arrangements for assessment, its recording and its reporting. OFSTED (1993) sets out several focuses for inspection in the area of assessment: accurate and comprehensive records; appropriacy of arrangements for assessment; outcomes of assessment to be useful to pupils, teachers, parents, employers; formative assessments; frequency and regularity of reports; consistency of reporting practice; frequency of reports to parents and for transfer; regularity of review of assessment procedures; staff discussion of records received. If the ten factors identified are addressed in the planning and implementation of assessment for the cross-curricular themes then these criteria should be covered automatically.

The special character of the cross-curricular themes is both a bonus and a problem. On the one hand their non-statutory status offers a far greater degree of flexibility in addressing assessments. If it is decided that assessment will be undertaken in these areas then there is a wide choice of what and how to assess, what to include and what to exclude. Further, because the cross-curricular themes are specified in terms of key stages rather than levels there is a built-in flexibility which can be used to advantage in assessing the cross-curricular themes. Assessment can be open-ended and can include self-reporting by students. The assessment can be recorded in experiential rather than measurable terms, ie assessors can break the hold over assessments which is currently kept by numbers, tick-boxes and the trappings of psychometry.

On the other hand there are several inherent difficulties in assessing the cross-curricular themes if the demands of validity and reliability are to be met. Because the teaching and learning of the cross-curricular themes are arguably broader than in the other subjects of the national curriculum, there are more factors to be addressed in developing assessments. For example a greater range of people, learning environments, types of resources, teaching and learning styles may be involved.

Because some of the work of the cross-curricular themes is undertaken out of school (involving different places, people, experiences) it is difficult to ensure parity of richness or experiences available to students in these out-of-school contexts. It could be argued that the community representatives ought to be involved in assessments. This would require a considerable amount of time in preparing the members of the community to be fair assessors and ensuring inter-rater reliability and the building out of bias. Involving outsiders in assessment might raise an immense problem of reliability; outsiders may need to be trained in assessment. Further, it will involve extensive moderation of results to ensure consistency of focuses, methods, criteria to be used (and their actual use), content, formats, level of detail, methods and standardisation of outcomes. Whilst some of these factors can be addressed by having assessments conform to school-given criteria and formats, the possibility for bias and subjectivity is still high. For example, assessors might be building in their own prejudices in assessing, the assessment telling more about the assessor than the assessed.

Law (1984) indicates very considerable problems in open-ended reporting as it may be (a) generalised, (b) unfairly impressionistic and biased, (c) based on hunch rather than evidence, (d) value-laden and (e) beyond the capability of the assessor to know the assessed in the depth which is indicated in the assessment. Hargreaves (1989) suggests that if local employers are involved in the devising and administration of assessments then this could skew the assessment towards it being a document for selection rather than motivational purposes. The data given for one set of purposes (motivation and a record of positive achievements) could be used for another set of purposes (employment selection).

It appears to go against the spirit of the themes to advance a single style of assessment which can be used uniformly for each theme. This may require assessment planners to indicate which aspects of the themes are common to each other and which are peculiar to each specific theme. To be faithful to each of the *Curriculum Guidance* documents very different factors for each theme should be the focuses of diagnosis. Time in schools is precious; the cross-curricular themes are collaborative and collective in nature. Hence there a question of how to assess the individual within a group and an issue of finding time to build and implement individual programmes in the cross-curriculum themes as a result of the diagnoses.

To summarise the position so far, assessment of the cross-curricular themes will need to address:

- the desirability of assessing students' achievements of the themes;
- whose interests are served by assessing students in the context of the themes;
- what and whose purposes are served by assessments of the themes;
- the focuses of assessments;
- the timing of assessments;
- particular issues of validity and reliability within a non-standardised form of assessment;
- the matching of tasks to students;
- issues of sampling and selection of assessment data;
- the criterion of 'fitness for purpose' in designing assessment instruments, methods of acquiring data, reporting and recording, with particular reference to assessment out of school;
- the criteria to be used in judging assessment data;

- the ethics of using assessment data;
- the constraints on diagnostic, formative, criterion-referenced assessments in terms of form and follow-up;
- the clarification of who to involve in the assessments;
- the need for assessment to be responsive to the particular character and contents of each *Curriculum Guidance* document;
- the need for assessments to be kept to a necessary minimum rather than to an unworkable maximum.
- the need for an open-ended and flexible form of assessment rather than a tick-sheet style of assessment.

Figure 5.1 – Written Sources of Assessment Data

WRITTEN SOURCES OF ASSESSMENT DATA		
METHOD	**STRENGTHS**	**WEAKNESSES**
Tests	Targeted, specific, written, flexible, marks can give credit and compensation for partial answers	Unnatural, threatening, outcome focused, Hawthorne effect, simplistic, only one 'correct' answer
Samples of work	Ongoing, part of everyday activities, May be representative	Need to ensure validity, Much hinges on single items, Problems for poor writers, Neglects processes
Records	Honest and cumulative, Specific and detailed	Time consuming, Risk of subjectivity
Questionnaires	Targeted, useful for gathering opinions, easy to process	Costly (time and money), problems for poor writers, off-putting, unreliable
Diaries	Ongoing, honest, cumulative, wide-ranging	Ethics of release of private data, irrelevant data, biased
Self-completed, self-referenced assessments	Honest, focused, highlights priorities, high ownership,	Problem for poor writers, Problem of institutional response only, irrelevant

Figure 5.2 – Non-written Sources of Assessment Data

NON-WRITTEN SOURCES OF ASSESSMENT DATA		
METHOD	STRENGTHS	WEAKNESSES
Observation (visual, aural)	Strong on reality, taken in context	Distracting for teacher, time-consuming
Practical activities – concrete outcome	Part of everyday work, motivating, active	Difficult to build out influence or contribution of others
Interviews and conferencing	Builds on known relationships, can be detailed, deep and focused	Time consuming to undertaken and to analyse, students are inhibited
Presentations	Economical on time as part of everyday work, good motivator	Students are inhibited
Video and audio recordings	Strong on reality, captures complexity, can suit poor writers	Time consuming to listen to and analyse, Hawthorne effect
Photographs	Records the non-written, wide focus	Selective, expensive, Freezes complexity

Making assessments practicable

The time available for assessment is limited and a high level of specificity is consequently impractical. This impacts on the nature of the instruments to be used for assessment purposes. Time is not available to undertake tasks simply for the purposes of assessment, hence assessment activities will have to be teaching and learning activities, 'built-in' rather than 'bolt-on'. The teacher has available to her a battery of assessment instruments. Figure 5.1 indicates written sources of assessment data and Figure 5.2 indicates non-written sources of assessment data. The particular strengths and weaknesses of each method are indicated.

These are the principal means of acquiring assessment evidence. It can be seen that many of these activities can be set into day-to-day teaching arrangements. This is particularly the case if those teaching arrangements are broadly based, active and experiential as these will involve the students in providing, gathering and recording data in a variety of forms. Whichever methods of acquiring information are used the teacher can then use the *Curriculum Guidance* documents to derive the criteria for assessing a student's achievements and performance. The selection of which methods to adopt for acquiring assessment evidence is underpinned by the criterion of 'fitness for purpose'. For example it might be of little value to apply a written test if the student has been involved in an essentially practical activity; rather the use of observational data or a discussion of the outcomes of the activity might be more valid.

The discussion so far has supposed that the assessments will be largely of an individual character. However the cross-curricular themes are explicit in their support of a group approach to projects. If a group approach has been adopted then a group assessment seems to be most appropriate. There are several ways in which a group project can be assessed, see Figure 5.3.

What is being suggested here is that group work will have an identifiable outcome or product. This can speak for itself though the teacher will need to target some specific questions to the group or the individuals in the group (which may mean devoting some additional time to individuals in addition to the group response) to ascertain the contribution of individuals and the processes which the group went through to reach the outcome. The outcome might be wide-ranging, for example a multi-media display, a multi-curriculum-area display, written work, graphs, photographs, drawings, paintings, objects, games, drama, folders of work, models, diagrams, newspapers, production of resources, a song etc., – the list is vast. The outcome might be an ongoing project, for instance a business mini-enterprise, a multi-media pack on the local environment, setting up a shop in the school, a pack about solvent abuse, arranging a visit to the local environment (including bringing in speakers to the school), setting up an advice bureau for careers or consumer affairs, keeping the local environment clean, having a classroom 'court' for keeping rules.

In these examples it might be neither desirable nor practicable to isolate an individual's contribution to a collective project as contributions might change over time, they might not be observable, they might be subtle or 'behind the scenes'. A group assessment, then, will select key points for comment.

When one examines the *Curriculum Guidance* documents it is clear that they have not been framed in criterion-specific terms. They are only loosely domain referenced (ie identifying a field) and related to key stages rather that to levels.[5] For example the document *Education for*

Figure 5.3 – Sources of Group Assessment Data

SOURCES OF GROUP ASSESSMENT DATA		
METHOD	STRENGTHS	WEAKNESSES
Observation (visual, aural)	Strong on reality, taken in context	Distracting for teacher time-consuming
Practical activities – concrete outcome	Part of everyday work, motivating, active	Difficult to build out influence or contribution of others
Interviews and conferencing	Builds on known relationships, can be detailed, deep and focused	Time consuming to undertaken and to analyse, students are inhibited
Group Presentations	Economical on time as part of everyday work, mutual group support, good motivator	Students are inhibited, difficult to discern individual student's contributions
Samples of work	Ongoing, part of everyday activities, May be representative	Need to ensure validity, Much hinges on single items, Problems for poor writers, Neglects processes
Video and audio recordings	Strong on reality, captures complexity, can suit poor writers	Time consuming to listen to and analyse, Hawthorne effect
Photographs	Records the non-written, wide focus	Selective, expensive, Freezes complexity, Neglects processes
Self-completed, self-referenced assessments	Honest, focused, highlights priorities, high ownership,	Problem for poor writers, Problem of institutional response only, irrelevant

Economic and Industrial Understanding suggests that students should have knowledge and understanding of 'key economic concepts, such as production, distribution, and supply and demand' (DES, 1990a, p. 4), or 'understand how some things are produced, using different resources' (ibid., p. 15). These are non-operational statements. It is impossible to state exactly what is required for the successful acquisition of these or to envisage a minimum set of contexts which would be necessary to ensure that students had learnt the message of these statements. It is hard to envisage or to identify what types of or actual, specific behaviours would be required of the students in order to demonstrate their achievements of these statements.

The implications of these characteristics are twofold. It could be seen as an open invitation to teachers to operationalise these statements into finer, more detailed and more progressive statements of objectives, furthering the behavioural objectives model. That is to violate the very flexibility of the *Curriculum Guidance* documents. Rather, it is to suggest that where statements are provided in the *Curriculum Guidance* documents they should be seen as *guidance* only, as defining a field upon which teachers and students can comment as deemed appropriate together with supporting evidence, dated and relating to specific experiences.

One should be mindful here of the Schools' Council (1981) definition of the effective curriculum as that which is taken away by each child (Schools Council, 1981, p. 42). It also reasserts the value of a simplistic view of assessment which asks: what do I know now, feel now and what can I do now that I did not or could not before I undertook the programme? This suggests that the overwhelming nature of assessment in the cross-curricular themes should be selective, avoiding a long list of competencies or an attempt to list every aspect of every theme as this suffers from an inability to differentiate the important from the trivial.

Recording assessments

Respecting the flexibility and generality of the *Curriculum Guidance* documents is to follow the pattern of the *Primary Language Record* (ILEA, 1989) in which key areas are defined, guideline phrases and sub-elements of each area are set out in minimal form only as an *aide-memoire,* and space for comments made available. The guideline phrases might be taken from the statements in the *Curriculum Guidance* documents, key concepts, key questions, key topic areas or project titles (discussed in chapter three).

Where links with the community are used and community representatives might be involved in assessment[6] – perhaps in work placements – a standardised format for assessment can enable some parity of recording to be undertaken together with comments from teachers and students themselves, for example Figure 5.4 (reduced from original size).

Figure 5.4 – Report Form for Work Experience

REPORT FORM FOR WORK EXPERIENCE	
Name	School
Period of work	Type of work
Effort	
Punctuality	
Self-discipline	
Perseverance	
Reliability	
Abilities in working with adults	
Initiative	
Adaptability	
Confidence	
Specific and particular skills	
Other observations	

Teachers and students should be assessing what the students 'got out of' a particular experience as well as recording the acquisition and application of a field of knowledge. This recognises that validity becomes reinterpreted as that which is defined as valid by teachers and students together as well as that which bears comparison with other assessments. This is to sideline the notions of moderation and concurrent validity and to argue that content validity is negotiable and should be negotiated because it derives from the students' views of validity and worthwhileness. It also recognises that teachers and students need not feel obliged to comment on every aspect of every theme, indeed the notion of selectivity is a useful way of identifying priorities and key features. This can feed directly into a Record of Achievement.

A planning document can also be used as a document of record. The headings and subtitles in the planning document − the teacher's record of planning − become the headings and subtitles in the document of record. These, together with suitable blank spaces introduced to allow room for comments, can be used as the assessment record.

What follows from the preceding discussion of assessment here suggests four components or stages of the assessment process and its recording.

Stage one involves the identification at the planning stage of the *terms* in which the cross-curricular theme(s) will be planned and how these will be set out in a document of record. This might include key concepts, key questions, a description of content, the statements from the *Curriculum Guidance* documents, particular activities, areas of knowledge, skills, attitudes. The document might take the form of a pamphlet for each theme, or sheets on a Record of Achievement.

Stage two involves the recording of appropriate *descriptive* evidence of coverage of the theme with reference to the terminology set out in stage one, dated to identify periods of rapid coverage and periods of consolidation. It records performance in terms of experiences met rather than measured achievements and thereby enables an open-ended response to be reported.

Stage three involves the recording of a *judgement* of value of the experiences, activities and progress. It identifies significant areas of experience, improvement, problems, concerns and enjoyments. In short it is an evaluation of that which the student has 'got out of' the area of the theme and learnt from it − the 'quality' of experience as indicated in the definition of assessment at the start of this chapter.

Stage four involves the setting of targets in light of the assessment made, ie *action planning* by the students and teachers to include new content, skills and experiences to be addressed, applications of existing knowledge, practice and consolidation of learnt materials, areas for deeper, further or broader study.

Several years ago a cartoon appeared in the national press which showed a group of bored and dishevelled young children standing in the pouring rain at Stonehenge; one child turned to another and commented ruefully that they would be expected to write about this upon their return to school. Extensive writing can be unnecessary, meaningless, purposeless and a certain demotivator for many students and many teachers. If a document is to be written then it must be kept to a minimum; recording everything is as unhelpful as recording nothing. After all, in everyday life we do not record everything that we experience. The need to record must be tempered by criteria of utility and worth. A photograph or picture might be just as informative as several pages of writing.

If teachers' professional judgement is to be respected then this will invite a recognition that an informal record, not necessarily greatly committed to paper, might be just as valuable as a vast quantity of undifferentiated reportage. Clearly this will be influenced by the audiences of the record. If it is for private consumption by an individual teacher then its nature and contents are an individual matter. If the record is for other teachers within the school or for the student and whomever she wishes to see it outside school then this might affect the format, range and contents. An example of the latter can be seen in Figure 5.5 (reduced from original size).

In this example the concepts which appear in the *Curriculum Guidance* document have been used to organise the record. In this case the main concepts have all been represented so that when entries are made it can be seen which concepts have been covered at some length and which have received less coverage. A second sheet could be made to cover *skills,* a third to cover *attitudes* and a fourth to cover *community involvement.* In this instance a four-side document could be sufficient for each child for each key stage. Though the *Curriculum Guidance* documents vary in their coverage of concepts, skills, attitudes, community involvement it is possible nevertheless to go through them and identify these four elements in each.

An alternative method is to cover the four elements in a different format. In the example of Figure 5.6 this has been undertaken for Education for Citizenship but the difference here is that no concepts, skills, attitudes or involvement with the community have been prespecified − that is for each teacher to write into the document of record. In the example of Figure 5.6 space has been provided for

Figure 5.5 – Recording Assessments for EIU

ASSESSMENT RECORD FOR EIU		
PROJECT / ACTIVITY		DATES
Concepts	Teachers' comments	Student's comments
Economic concepts		
Business Enterprise		
Industry and Work		
Consumer Affairs		
Government and Society		
Particular points to note		
Points for future		

teachers and students to comment, for specific points to be made, and for forward planning to be undertaken. For many students a blank page elicits a blank response, so teachers will have to be prepared with questions, prompts and probes for students in opening up a discussion.

Figure 5.6 – Recording Achievements in Education for Citizenship

ASSESSMENT RECORD FOR CITIZENSHIP EDUCATION	
Dates	Project / Activity / Area of Study
Concepts: Teacher's comments: Student's comments:	
Skills: Teacher's comments: Student's comments:	
Attitudes: Teacher's comments: Student's comments:	
Community Involvement: Teacher's comments: Student's comments:	
Future points:	

Being realistic, because of the time constraints operating on the cross-curricular themes, teachers' formal and recorded assessments of students' achievements of the cross-curricular themes are likely to be limited and could rely on recollections written very shortly after the events. That being the case it is unwise to expect to include more details than the examples above provide unless specific students or specific aspects of the themes have been targeted for extended and detailed assessment for a specific purpose.

The overwhelming message of this chapter is this: *in approaching assessments of students' achievements of the cross-curricular themes, it is the teacher's familiarity with the contents of the* Curriculum Guidance *documents which is the fundamedal factor so that she can selectively address from the documents those elements which she considers to be the significant aspects of a student's progress.* That respects teachers' professionalism in terms of having a working knowledge of the documents and in terms of using professional insights into the students' abilities to know what is and what is not worth recording. This suggestion relies very heavily on teachers' judgements; it risks the problems of subjectivity and potential bias in teachers, it risks the open-ended word-based recording that tells more about the teacher than the student. However these are matters for professional development rather than arguments to support tick sheets, surveillance and endless interrogation of students.

Summary

This chapter has exposed some fundamental concerns about assessment within the context of the national curriculum and, therefore, as applied to the cross-curricular themes. The particular nature of the cross-curricular themes – their low status, the flexibility of their framing, the experiential nature of their learning – were seen to raise specific issues in the designing, implementation and recording of assessments. A range of issues to be considered in the designing and implementation of assessments was indicated, and the instrumentation for gathering assessment data was discussed. A recurrent feature of this chapter has been the partnership between teacher-determined and student-determined assessment. The case was made for student-determined contents and focuses of assessments and their recording. This is to be coupled with a minimal but representatively selective sampling of students' achievements in concept, skill and attitude formation and experiences in community involvement.

The need for a realistic appraisal of time pressures and the inherent flexibility and open-endedness of the cross-curricular themes argued against extensive assessment and in favour of a selective written set of comments. This hinged on and respected teachers' knowledge of the criteria for assessment which are set out in the *Curriculum Guidance* documents. The culmination of this argument is to suggest that an open-ended, flexible, jointly owned assessment (by the teachers and students) is the most accessible and practicable means of addressing the concerns which were voiced about assessment in the national curriculum in the early sections of this chapter. The message was to turn away from ticksheets and competency models of assessment towards selective and qualitative assessments.

Notes

1. Apple (1993a) comments on a similar situation occurring in the USA in the proposals for a form of national curriculum intended to raise standards.

2. The Hawthorne effect means that simply putting students into an assessment situation will cause their behaviour and achievements to alter. For a discussion of the research which led to this term see Hughes, (1976, pp. 94–97). See also Bowring-Carr (1993).

3. For the national curriculum this will be approached by moderating work (DFE, Circular 11 / 93, p. 7) internally with reference to a school portfolio of examples of work assessed and agreed for every level of every attainment target for every subject with reference to which an individual child's portfolio can be assembled and updated (SCAA, 1993b).

4. A very full critique of reliability is provided by Nuttall (1988) and Cresswell and Houghton (1991).

5. For a discussion of domain referencing see Wiliam (1993).

6. This is mooted by OFSTED (1993).

CHAPTER SIX

Cross-Curricular Themes As Innovations

Introduction

This chapter argues that the cross-curricular themes constitute a lever of massive change in schools. They herald changes to curriculum aims, content, pedagogy, assessment and recording, ethos, interpersonal relationships and management structures. The nature of these changes will be explored. For the purposes of this chapter it is immaterial to distinguish between change and innovation. Some changes and innovations are relatively superficial, rendering the *existing* system more efficient – a first order change in content. Other changes and innovations are more fundamental – second order changes which alter and replace systems, roles, cultures and structures rather than fine tuning them (Cuban, 1990).

This chapter will argue that the implementation of the cross-curricular themes can be handled well if they become part of the school development plan, and it will demonstrate how this can occur. The preceding chapters have indicated that a major concern in curriculum planning for cross-curricular themes is an elevation of their status. Hence successful planning and implementation will have to ensure that their status is raised and that the significance of this for the whole school is realised in planning and implementation.

Clarifying the components of change

Change and innovation are no strangers to schools at present. The introduction of the national curriculum has brought massive changes to schools. Many teachers are suffering from 'innovation fatigue'. The strain of having to cope with multiple changes in telescoped time scales and with finite resources is telling in their reluctance to undertake any more innovations than are absolutely necessary. In this respect the implementation of a non-statutory element of the national curriculum is almost certain to bring with it a hostility to yet more change. It is perceived to have a low priority even though it brings with it perhaps more fundamental changes that many teachers will have encountered to date. The implementation of the cross-curricular themes represent a fundamental shift of practices in schools. Like Records of Achievement the cross-curricular themes can be regarded as levers of change – specific innovations which have a 'knock-on' effect, bringing major changes in schools. This can be demonstrated by examining the 'knock-on' effects of introducing this specific innovation thus:

- it has been suggested in the preceding chapters that the cross-curricular themes will touch every other curricular area;
- to do justice to the cross-curricular themes will require an elevation of their status;
- elevating their status will require changes to all other areas of the curriculum in terms of content, pedagogy and timetabling;
- attention to content and pedagogy will involve cross-phase, cross-department, cross-faculty planning as the implementation of cross-curricular themes requires whole-school approaches to be adopted;
- whole-school approaches require attention to flexible timetabling of the school day, week, term and year;
- whole-school planning which involves flexible timetabling will involve opening up channels of communication between teachers in all areas of the school;
- opening up all areas of the school to scrutiny and rationalisation will challenge some teachers' traditional practices and beliefs;
- challenging teachers' practices and beliefs will constitute challenging the whole school's ethos.

The suggestion is that change and innovation for the implementation of cross-curricular themes be regarded as fundamental rather than superficial (Cuban's second order change). This echoes Hoyle's (1975) comment where he writes that curriculum innovation will require change in the internal organisation of the school and that changing the internal organisation of the school itself is a major innovation (Hoyle, 1975).

Hoyle is pointing to perhaps the most significant aspect of change, *viz.* that shifting practices is much easier to accomplish than shifting structures. Indeed he suggests that successful change is a function of the extent to which attention has been paid to the idiographic (person-centred) aspects of change as well as the nomothetic aspects of change (norms, structures, roles in the institution). One can distil from the international literature on change, with its pedigree from the 1970s onwards[1] several recommendations for regarding change:

- change is fundamental, systemic and system disturbing;
- change is a multi-dimensional phenomenon;
- change is a process over time, not a single event; different processes take different lengths of time;
- change is as much about people as it is about curriculum content;
- conflict and disagreement are inevitable to change;
- successful change requires attention to organisational health and organisational climate;
- change is most successful where it is collectively 'owned';
- change is most successful when it is a visible response to a perceived need from participants and where it is seen to empower participants;
- strategies of change and dissemination have to be planned;
- attention has to be given to the management of change as much as to its content;
- assume not only that people need pressure to change but that not everybody will be able to change;
- assume that changing the culture of an institution is the real agenda rather than simply introducing single innovations;
- assume that *behaviour* changes before *beliefs* (ie start small but think big!);
- communication, consultation, leadership and involvement are vital ingredients of successful change.

These messages are not new, indeed they are currently played out on a daily basis in most schools since the onset of the national curriculum. This chapter and the next will address these issues and make recommendations for practice. Given the size and scope of the discussion of change this chapter will proceed by outlining factors which inhibit change and factors which facilitate change, and indicate how these might be addressed in implementing the cross-curricular themes.

Planning for change

What is required is an audit of the existing situation in the institution in order to identify its potential to take on yet more changes and innovations. An early part of the audit will examine the several factors which contribute towards successful change and identify barriers to change so that ways of overcoming them can be addressed.

Dalin (1978) suggests four categories of barrier to successful change: value, power, practical and psychological barriers. Each of these barriers has its component elements thus:

- *Value barriers:* different people have their own constructions of worthwhileness, therefore conflict and disagreement over the value or extent of the innovation are endemic.

Indeed Huberman and Miles (1984) and Fullan (1991) suggest that if an innovation is going smoothly then this is an indication that very little is actually changing. Superficial changes (Cuban's *first order* changes) are often more successful than second order changes simply because they *are* superficial and do not require attention to value barriers. Indeed Davis (1983) suggests that changing the patterns of group beliefs and behaviours are amongst the most long-term aspects of change. The rule of thumb here is that the more fundamental is the change the longer it might take to become institutionalised. Hence one task of the curriculum planner is to place aspects of the innovation on a continuum from the superficial to the fundamental, to indicate the time scales for each element and to identify where ideological disagreements might be found.

Of course this *gradualist* approach to innovation might not fully embrace the fundamental nature of the innovation. For example, though the introduction of the cross-curricular themes might be trialled with a limited number of teachers covering limited aspects of the themes, it might not be feasible to introduce the cross-curricular themes gradually because they have so many 'knock-on' effects. Rather, it might be the case that a very considerable amount of time has to be spent in planning the content, pedagogy, management, assessment, resourcing, time-tabling, organization etc. but that it will be the case that from the first day of the new school year this new initiative will be implemented lock, stock and barrel. In that way though the disturbance to the system is huge, it is confined to a small amount of time. That might be the lesser of two evils! It has its parallel in school closures and amalgamations where, for example, two schools (eg an infant and a junior school) close on one day and open on the next day as a new combined school.

- *Power barriers:* people will resist an innovation which redistributes power in the institution as it threatens the power of some teachers whilst extending the power of others.

There are instances where what appear to individuals be value barriers turn out to be power barriers. For example the head of a history department might suddenly find that her power has been superseded by the introduction of a head of a faculty of humanities under the guise of creating faculties in the institution to rationalise resource allocation and to provide a collective identity for particular groups of subjects.

- *Practical barriers:* the size and scope of the change might throw up immense practical difficulties, for example:

(i)   an increase in teachers' workload in developing the new curriculum;
(ii)   a loss of teachers' self-confidence as innovations often bring a deskilling element (eg teachers being asked to teach content for which they have no expertise);
(iii) teachers' reluctance to become reskilled (maybe because of an ideological disagreement with the proposed change, maybe because of increased workload, maybe because of the stage in a teacher's career in which they no longer wish to continue to innovate);
(iv)   lack of resources – human, temporal, material, spatial, administrative, financial, expertise, supportive, organizational (discipline, classes and groupings, timetabling, specialist facilities, physical, storage, architectural).

This issue brings a sense of realism which tempers the possibilitarian tone of many curriculum planners. It requires planners to be clear about what actually can be managed in a specific institution at a specific point of time with specific resources and with a specific group of teachers whose workloads are already at breaking point.

- *Psychological barriers:* there is a tendency for individuals to resist change because it is unsettling and because it requires additional resources of motivation in an age of public accountability. Teachers are reluctant to discard tried and tested ways of working, they might see that they are simply advancing the careers of others at their own expense.

Change is threatening and, faced with threat, teachers might adopt the flight or fight coping strategies, either of which constitutes a threat to the success of change.

From the literature on change one can identify several properties of unsuccessful or only partially successful innovations:

- lack of clarity in identifying the components of the innovation;
- an oversimplification of the change, making it appear less complex that in fact it is;
- a reluctance to face up to or to communicate the complexity of the change;
- unrealistic time perspectives;
- too great a disjunction between established and proposed practices and the principles on which these are based (ie the question of *consonance);*

- an unrealistic expectation of the practical commitment required by teachers, eg in terms of workload, reskilling, planning time, values etc.;
- absence of monitoring procedures;
- absence or underestimation of required resources;
- lack of collegiality and a collaborative culture;
- lack of incentives to change.

These will suggest their own several implications for successful introduction of the cross-curricular themes. One can detect in these an identification of significant components of change:

- the *content* of the innovation;
- the *people* involved;
- the *organizational health* of the institution;
- an *audit* of the existing and proposed situation;
- the support and resource implications of the innovation, ie the *management* of the innovation.

These five areas will be considered below.

The content of the innovation

In relation to the *content* of the innovation itself it appears that success of the innovation is related to a variety of factors: the communicability and clarity of the proposals; the potential for trialling (ie partialising the numbers of staff involved in the first instance); the potential for post-trial refinement of the proposal; the complexity of the proposals and their divisibility (ie partialising the proposals so that small sections of the proposals can be trialled); the compatibility with existing practices, ethos and values; the relative advantage of the proposal over existing practices; the resource support for the innovation; the clarity of the proposed innovation.

People involved in the innovation

In terms of the *people* involved in an innovation Hall and Hord (1987) set out their Concerns Based Adoption Model of change from the 1970s. Although this is more suited to a research, development and diffusion model of curriculum planning (eg an externally generated project), neverthless it makes it quite clear that significant attention must be paid to the participants in an innovation. They suggest that there are seven 'stages of concern' of individuals involved in curriculum innovations:

(i)   *awareness* of the innovation;

(ii) *informational* – a general awareness and concern for more information;

(iii) *personal* – a concern for how the innovation will impact on the individual and whether s/he is able to meet its demands;

(iv) *management* – concern about the organisational aspects of the innovation;

(v)   *consequence* – concern for how the innovation will impact on students;

(vi) *collaboration* – concern for how the innovation will be developed and managed with other colleagues;

(vii) *refocusing* – concern for developing beyond the proposed innovation.

The authors suggest that the typical model of concerns is that the lower orders of the hierarchy (awareness, information and a concern for how the innovation will affect the specific teacher) are met early in an innovation. The medium order concerns (personal, consequence, collaboration) are met once the innovation has begun to be planned or implemented. The later concern (refocusing) typically is raised once the innovation has been implemented and institutionalised for some time. This model has value in that it directs planners to take seriously the anxieties, interests and concerns of the participants. It also builds on and expands the suggestion that innovation concerns people as well as substantive contents.

The organizational health of the institution

In terms of *organizational health* of the institution the literature[2] suggests that an innovation is likely to be successful if it takes place in an organisation whose health is robust. Indeed OFSTED (1993) include the ethos and sense of purpose in a school as being important focuses for inspection. We can extend an analogy from Hoyle (1975) in discussing innovations: if one were to be involved in organ transplant surgery not only would the donor organ have to be of a high quality and well matched to the individual receiving it, but the recipient's body would have to be prepared in order that 'tissue rejection' might be avoided. So it is in innovation. The health of the school must be such that it will be able to accept changes and innovations. What are the characteristics of an organisationally healthy institution?

The international literature on successful innovation[2] indicates a level of agreement amongst writers about the key factors of organisational health. The aspects of these that relate to innovation can be presented as in Figure 6.1.

Figure 6.1 – Characteristics of Organizational Health

CHARACTERISTICS OF ORGANIZATIONAL HEALTH	
COMMUNICATION	Open and utilised vertical and lateral channels of communication; consultation;
SUPPORT	Support (in all forms) for risk taking institutionally and in networks of institutions; institutional integrity; resource support; resource utilization – a balance between overload and idling;
MORALE	High morale; motivation; cohesiveness and loyalty to an institution;
INNOVATIVENESS	A tradition of innovating and creativity; collegial planning; problem-solving adequacy – a usedness to solving problems with minimal exertion of effort; teachers operating as 'extended professionals'; autonomy of the institution to mediate external demands for innovation;
LEADERSHIP	A clear goal focus; open and consultative, sharing decition making and respecting autonomy; respecting personal welfare of individuals and sharing power equitably.

One can see in this figure a concern for people, processes and management in addition to the ability of the organisation to take on the substance of an innovation. What is clear also is that organisational health is met both in the outcome and process of innovation. If organisational health is to be fostered then being involved in innovations could promote this.

Auditing the curriculum

In terms of an *audit* of the present and proposed situations a situational analysis will identify the facilitating and constraining factors in the

132

school which have a bearing on the success of planning and implementing the cross-curricular themes. Morrison (1992) identifies factors which might facilitate or inhibit change with regard to the development and the implementation of the cross-curricular themes, regardless of schools, age phases and curriculum areas taught (Figure 6.2).

Figure 6.2 – Factors which Facilitate and Impede Innovation

| FACTORS WHICH FACILITATE AND IMPEDE INNOVATION ||
Facilitating Factors	Impeding Factors
Good relationships between staff	Poor relationships between staff; private agendas
Open, sharing, cooperative school ethos; teamwork; reporting to colleagues	Poor ethos; lack of coordination
Framework for development; clear aims	Little forward planning
Resource support (in many forms)	Few resources; no 'prime time' for planning
Raising status; using promoted posts; appointing effective leader	Curriculum overload and little prioritisation; appointing ineffective leader; negative reactions from senior / middle management and outside agencies
Appropriate methods of delivery; acquisition of new skills; community links; opportunity to work in new teams	People forced into involvement; Reluctance to move away from subject divisions
Agreement on what is achievable	Swamping participants with too many innovations
Appropriate level of in-service support	No time given for staff development
Triallability – plan, teach, review	Too much to do by too many people in too short a time scale

What can be seen very clearly from this brief list is that these main features of innovation resonate with the preceding discussion of organisational health. They suggest the need for innovations to pay attention to individuals and the need to identify the barriers to innovation which exist in the school. The use of Delphi techniques and nominal group techniques (discussed in chapter eight) can play a significant part in accomplishing a quick audit of present circumstances.[3]

The management of the innovation

In terms of the *management* of the innovation it is clear from the preceding discussion that the successful management of the innovation will have commenced long before the specific innovation is mooted, for it will have involved the establishment of an organisational climate which is conducive to innovation. This will involve open planning, cooperative styles of development and effective leadership styles. The leader will have an overview of the whole innovation and will be open to consultation about the planning and implementation of the innovation. The leader will have an earned status in the school (ie possessing credibility and legitimacy), and will be capable of coordinating teams and organizing the development of the innovation. The nature of teams and effective leadership are discussed in the next chapter.

The management of the innovation will link with the strategies of innovation which can be employed. The preceding discussion has indicated that one inescapable element of innovation is the assumption of conflict and disagreement. The successful management of conflict is a function not only of the personalities involved but of the strategies which are employed to build in and build on the support of participants. Some strategies seek to persuade by the force of argument and evidence – taking people by the heart and the mind from one set of beliefs and practices to another. Alternatively, others adopt a more coercive tack, proceeding by the force of positional power in the face of resistances – taking people by the hair in the knowledge that hearts and minds might or might not follow but that changing behaviour almost certainly will. Clearly it is impossible to prescribe in a context-free manner when and where different strategies will be employed, that is a matter for the specific institution. The former strategies are sympathetic to a collegial, democratic style of decision making and curriculum development, the latter might be indicative of necessary autocracy. The management of the development of cross-curricular themes will involve addressing a value barrier. It will have to persuade participants that the cross-curriculum themes are essential and central features of the curriculum, no simply optional extras, and that they articulate with major features of society outside and beyond school.

The appointment of a senior member of staff with clear and visible responsibility for the cross-curricular themes and where these feature highly on that person's list of priorities will enable power barriers to be

134

addressed. However this might be to anticipate an oppositional and confrontational approach to management, keeping a coercive strategy in the wings ready to be brought into the arena when disagreements occur. The signals which could be given by the appointment of a senior member of staff with this responsibility might be counter-productive. On the other hand not to designate responsibility for the cross-curricular themes to a senior member of staff might be to reaffirm their low status. Clearly it is a sensitive management task to indicate that the appointment of a senior member of staff with responsibility for the development of the cross-curricular themes is a recognition of the importance of the themes rather than in anticipation of resistance. This is a major issue which will receive extended treatment in the next chapter.

The management of the innovation will have to address the set of practical issues in the development of cross-curricular themes. One of the major management tasks will be to ensure that plentiful resources are available for the development of the initiative. The innovation is not to be managed on a shoestring because it is too important to risk failure. Significant material resources will have to be forthcoming if the cross-curricular themes are to be developed. With the rise of LMS the decision to finance the cross-curricular themes considerably will not be painless. However not to do so will quickly exhaust the goodwill of staff who are being asked to involve themselves in developing a non-statutory innovation. Given that one of the barriers to change is psychological then attention to the provision of appropriate resources will be an important feature of sustaining motivation and generating incentives for staff to become involved in the innovation.

In terms of time management the management of the innovation will involve ensuring that *curriculum development time* is build into the school calendar so that teachers can be released to work in cross-phase, cross-subject and cross-faculty teams. It will also involve ensuring that *staff development time* is built in the school calendar and development plan. This recognizes that deskilling and reskilling are unavoidable elements. Further, it accords status to the cross-curricular themes by releasing staff to be involved in the development of expertise in these areas. The management of the innovation will also involve *resource development time* so that high quality resources can be requisitioned and brought into the planning of curricula. Resource development will also involve planning and strengthening community links and environmental resources.

It was suggested earlier that the implementation of the cross-curricular themes was a fundamental rather than a superficial change.

Recognising this will means that *management development time* will have to be included in planning. This will mean releasing team leaders, heads of department, co-ordinators, faculty heads as appropriate from other tasks in order to enable team development to be advanced. The development of teams is a major feature which will be discussed more fully in the next chapter. At this point it is necessary to indicate that this cannot take place on an *ad hoc* arrangement; rather it will need to be programmed into the time frames and school development plan for the year. That could be one of the tasks of the senior leader of the curriculum innovation.

Time will need to be made available for development activities. Such time should not be after school as extra activities as this automatically signals its marginal position. Rather it should be during the school day as part of course development which is at the heart of school planning. Important timetabling decisions will have to be taken so that staff can be released. This is no more than the operation of an industrial model of education which has been much vaunted by successive governments, wherein planning and development time does not take place out of hours but is the first item to be programmed into the calendar of events. With regard to schools this means that development time might be the first item to be put into the calendar for the school year, term, week and day. This is not simply to compound managerialism in education, it is to recognise that if students are to receive high quality education then this should be planned during high quality time, not after school or at the end of a term when teachers typically are exhausted. Not to do this will result in furthering the view that teachers inflict wounds on themselves, eroding their own working conditions and their freedoms outside the workplace.

What is being advocated here is that if *total* quality management is to be addressed in school then this totality will embrace the several elements of school resource management.

The management of the innovation will also need to address the *strategy* to be involved in the curriculum development. Whilst the statutory elements of the national curriculum are premissed largely on a research, development and diffusion model which has been externally generated and put into schools by a top-down strategy with the force of law, the case of the cross-curricular themes is very different. The responsibility for their development is the province of schools, with only curriculum guidance provided by the National Curriculum Council.

This is to suggest that there is considerably more flexibility in planning for the cross-curricular themes than in other areas of the curriculum. It means that problem-solving, 'bottom-up' approaches can be adopted in curriculum development of the cross-curricular themes wherein teachers themselves identify the problems in developing and implementing the themes and, together, work towards their solution. This can make for greater staff commitment, involvement and ownership. This approach also ensures that the purposes, contents and objectives of the innovation are made very clear to participants because it is they who are working to clarify them. Cross-curricular themes, then, can be tailored very specifically to schools. This is itself a feature which addresses the need for as great a level of consonance between existing practices in the school and proposed developments to be maintained.

Because time scales are not specified for the introduction of the cross-curricular themes this enables sections of the curriculum development to be isolated (the issue of *divisibility)* and trialled (the issue of *triallability)*. Because there is less prescription in the cross-curricular themes the decisions on the implementation of the themes can be taken collectively and collegially. This furthers the development of open and democratic decision making in a culture of collaboration. In turn this contributes to the development of sound organisational health and a positive organisational climate.

What is being suggested here is that the management of the development of the cross-curricular themes will maximise the opportunities in them for flexibility and for addressing the several features of successful curriculum innovation.

School development plans

The preceding discussion has suggested that the introduction and implementation of the cross-curricular themes constitutes a major and complex innovation and that the management of this innovation will be a significant factor its success. Manageability is the key to the planning and implementation of this innovation. Faced with a project of immense size like this, one way in which to approach the task is to identify (a) which parts of the innovation can be put into smaller parcels, (b) which parts require handling on a whole school basis and (c) which parts can be addressed by a small team which is drawn from across the school. The notion of teams is explored in chapter seven. This chapter will argue that a useful way of rendering the planning and implementation of the cross-curricular themes manageable is through the use of school development plans. Indeed school development plans are scrutinised as part of a school's four-yearly inspection (OFSTED, 1993).

Essentially a school development plan is a managerial device for ensuring that aims and objectives of curricula and their organisation are translated into practice and subsequently evaluated. This can be done by:

- an audit of the present situation;
- the construction of an *action plan* to introduce new items into the school;
- putting the action plan into *practice;*
- the evaluation of the action plan and its implementation.

The notion of school development planning can be put into a cycle of events where the four elements above are met in the order set out here. After the evaluation has taken place a new cycle of audit, planning, implementation and evaluation is undertaken so that the innovation is regenerative. The cyclical and recyclical pattern of the school development plan echoes the Stages of Concern model of change outlined earlier (Hall and Hord, 1987) where they indicate that the most developed stage of concern is *refocusing,* where developments beyond the original intentions or plans are addressed by participants in an innovation.

The first stage of the school development plan is an *audit* of the existing situation in the school. This enables participants to identify areas of consonance between existing and proposed changes, itself a significant factor in the success of innovations. It exposes resistances, value barriers and resource implications. It indicates those areas where most change will have to occur if the innovation is to be successful. It enables participants to see with greater clarity those elements of the innovation which already exist (ie to enable *maintenance* of the situation to be identified) and those elements of the innovation which would have to be brought in *ab initio* (ie *development* tasks). It was suggested earlier that clarity of perception was a marked factor in the success of innovations. An audit should build on the preceding discussion of change, ie it should be not only in curriculum-specific terms but should include:

- organisational health and climate;
- openness to and tradition of change;
- identification of barriers to change and ways of addressing and overcoming them;
- identification of the features of the curriculum, the organisation of staff, resources and curricula;
- roles and relationships;
- identification of major characteristics of the innovation (eg its size, complexity, rate of change, degree of change – superficial to radical).

138

From an audit of the existing situation the *action plan* can then be constructed which will address:

- the setting into order of major to minor priorities;
- the setting of time scales for these priorities, ie putting the elements of an action plan into a temporal sequence – long term, medium term, short term;
- indicating how the low to high order priorities, set into a time sequence, will be put into practice. Hargreaves and Hopkins (1991) name this as the setting of 'routes' and 'tasks' for the implementation of the school development plans;
- identifying how the tasks will be commenced. Hargreaves and Hopkins (1991) name this as identifying the 'initial tasks';
- identifying who will be involved at the different stages of the plan, ie mapping the organisation of people onto the organisation of tasks which have been put into a chronology;
- identifying the 'success criteria' (Hargreaves and Hopkins, 1991) for the achievement of the short, medium and long term targets;
- identifying where the changes proposed by the innovation are new and where they can build on existing practices (ie root and branch planning respectively).

By building into an action plan a set of objectives and success criteria the criteria for evaluating the implementation and outcomes of the plan will have been identified. The identification of tasks, people and chronological sequence will clarify and break down the overall innovation into manageable units (the issues of divisibility). Hence the complexity of the innovation will have been rendered transparent, itself a significant factor in the success of an innovation.

It was suggested earlier that there was a high measure of flexibility in organizing the planning and implementation of the cross-curricular themes. Flexibility means that within a school development plan, the areas of development and implementation outlined in the previous chapters will be negotiable *viz:*

- the approaches to the planning of the content of the themes; (eg by objectives, permeation, key concepts, key questions, cross-subject topics, theme-specific topics);
- the planning of the organization of the content (eg permeation, as part of PSE, as a separately timetabled subject, as part of a pastoral programme, long block timetabling, flexible learning, resource-based learning);
- the planning of the pedagogical styles to be used for specific

elements of the themes (eg experiential, student-organised, didactic).

Additionally the school development plan will need to clarify the introduction of the cross-curricular themes. For example, decisions will have to be taken on whether to introduce the themes one at a time or simultaneously.

Introducing one theme at a time might possess the attraction of piloting, the avoidance of overload on staff and the possibility of building resources over time. However this approach means that it will take a long time before all of themes are in place in the curriculum. Further, the interrelationships between the themes might be lost and the curriculum will have to be constantly modified as each theme is introduced. Cross-curricularity might be jeopardised in this approach, the themes becoming marginal, bolt-on elements of the curriculum.

On the other hand there are strengths and weaknesses in bringing in all of the cross-curricular themes simultaneously. This approach has the attraction of making all of the changes in one fell swoop. It enables genuine cross-curricularity to be implemented from the very beginning and thereby ensures that the themes do not simply become bolt-on elements of the curiculum. It will be likely to involve all staff at the commencement of the exercise. However this approach takes a great deal of planning and preparation. It can risk becoming bogged down because of the complexity of the innovation and the level of co-ordination required for the exercise to be successful. Moreover the size of the undertaking might risk raising psychological barriers as staff feel overwhelmed. The success of this approach is a function of the size of the staff, the organisational health of the institution, and the establishing and co-ordination of teams.

There is considerable advantage in having only a few individuals or one small group of staff involved at first on a limited content area of the innovation as this enables piloting to be undertaken. Others will be able to learn from the experience. However this may mean that it might take a long time before all of the themes are implemented by all of the staff. A gradualist approach risks the disadvantages of delay.

Moreover, the nature of the dissemination, discussion and further development of the innovation might also be problematical in this instance. It might be seen, for example, that building on the experience of a few is to build on the work of an unrepresentative group in the school. Small scale innovation must be able to inform larger scale projects and feed into decision making if it is to be effective. It must be seen as important and a valuable piece of the innovation jigsaw if it is to have any real effect.

If several groups or the whole staff are involved this will have the attraction of having to address the systemic nature of the change and will expose the various facets of the innovation as indicated in the early part of this chapter. The time spent in co-ordinated meetings, feedback sessions, development meetings and resource preparation will be considerable. However it will have the advantage of ownership and involvement, a democratic approach to problem-solving, and a high possibility of ensuring the organisational health of the institution. On the other hand this approach will require considerable planning time and the identification of teams to work on different tasks with another tier of teams to maintain an overview and co-ordination role. This approach is 'front-loaded', taking much time to plan but subsequently little time to implement.

Conclusion

What emerges from the discussion so far confirms the value of a school development plan for turning aspirations into specific tasks. It also suggests that there is sufficient flexibility within the framework of school development plans for justice to be done to the development of cross-curricular themes. The framework of a school development plan is a ladder rather than a cage. It has been suggested that implementing the school development plan will require an identification of how teams will operate, what their tasks will be and how their work and its impact on students can be evaluated. Chapter seven indicates how this might be approached.

This chapter has argued that the implementation of the cross-curricular themes should be regarded as a lever of massive change because it is complex, multi-dimensional, systemic and faces a range of barriers to innovation that are present typically in large scale innovations. It was suggested that school development plans, themselves levers of change, could rationalise the development and implementation of the cross-curricular themes. It has suggested that because the introduction of cross-curricular themes possessed a high measure of flexibility this would enable time management to be fully addressed. Not only should quality time be used for planning but school development plans require forward planning to be taken seriously, a view reinforced by OFSTED, 1993. It was argued that the top-down approaches to curriculum innovation, wherein schools would have to interpret and tailor the substance of the *Curriculum Guidance* documents, can be complemented by a bottom-up problem-solving model of development through school development planning.

Giving charge of the development of the cross-curricular themes into the hands of teachers is not only a means to develop ownership through involvement but is a means of developing empowered teachers and empowered schools.[4] It was suggested that teacher empowerment was served well by the use of team planning and implementation. This is a crucial area of the development of cross-curricular themes and becomes the opening part of the next chapter.

Notes

1. For example, the work of Havelock (1973); Stenhouse (1975); Hoyle (1975); Miles (1975); Dalin (1978); Dalin and Rust (1983); Lieberman (1990); Fullan (1991); Dalin, Rolff and Kleekamp, (1993).

2. For example, Hoyle (1975); Miles (1975); Dalin and Rust (1983); Hoy *et al* (1990); Fullan (1991); Dalin, Rolff and Kleekamp (1993).

3. Elliott-Kemp and Williams (1979) have developed a quick-to-use instrument for evaluating the organisational health of an institution. See also Wilcox (1992) and Morrison (1993).

4. It is no accident, perhaps, that Hargreaves' and Hopkins' book about school development plans is titled *The Empowered School.*

CHAPTER SEVEN

Teamwork and Leadership

Introduction

The last chapter introduced the notion of school development planning and suggested that fundamental to the success of this was the commitment to team work. However, to devolve everything onto teams might be to dissipate responsibility for the development of the cross-curricular themes. It might be advisable to ensure that one team (or indeed one person) has an overview and a vision of the end state of the implementation of the themes. This chapter deals with two main managerial features – teamwork in and leadership of the development and implementation of the cross-curricular themes.

The need for teamwork

The *Curriculum Guidance* documents advocate very strongly the use of team approaches to planning and implementing the cross-curricular themes. Additionally there are very many reasons why team work should be a *requirement* of the planning and implementation of cross-curricular themes:

● it promotes organisational health;
● it empowers teachers;
● it rationalises workloads;
● it builds in democracy;
● it is an effective strategy for curriculum development;
● it is a feature of human interaction;
● it is fitting for the cross-curricular nature of the themes;
● every teacher in the school is affected by the development of the cross-curricular themes;
● it accords status to the cross-curricular themes.

The literature used in the previous chapter indicated that the organisational health of the institution was a vital ingredient for successful change. The notion of teamwork addresses those specific characteristics of organisational health which are summed up as *communication adequacy, optimal power equalisation, resource utilisation, cohesiveness, morale* and *problem-solving adequacy* (Miles, 1975). Indeed as a management strategy for developing and implementing innovation there has been a consistent message from the literature on innovation that team approaches are of great benefit in the field of innovation generally.[1] The previous chapter cited one significant barrier to change as the problem of overload which leads to innovation fatigue. The development of team approaches planning and implementation enables a division of labour to be undertaken in an attempt to keep teachers' workloads as manageable as possible.

The previous chapter dwelt on the fact that the planning and implementation of the cross-curricular themes constitutes a major, systemic change which touches everybody. If nobody can opt out, and if everyone's voice is to be given the opportunity to be heard then a mechanism has to be found of involving everybody and, at the same time, moving forward in the development of the themes. Too large a forum can lead to delay and the obfuscation of priorities; too small a forum can lead to the promotion or denial of sectional interests. The development of teams who are accountable and responsible to each other for a collective and collaborative enterprise is a powerful political force against demagogy and autocracy in the micropolitics of schools. In several schools the notion of teamwork itself will constitute a major innovation, echoing Hoyle's (1975) comment in the previous chapter that changing the internal structure of the school might be the largest innovation to be undertaken before curriculum innovation can be addressed.

Teamwork in practice

That the cross-curriculum themes cross the curriculum is a tautology. Nevertheless this carries a significant message for planning and implementing the cross-curricular themes. It suggests the *need* for teams, that the membership of each team should comprise staff from different age phases, different subjects, departments and faculties (where appropriate), different specialisms and areas of expertise, different positions in a hierarchy of promoted posts and areas of responsibility. Curriculum planners have at their disposal a wide range of items that must be 'crossed' if cross-curricularity is to be effected. Whilst this might be desirable it has to be tempered with reality or else every member of staff will be on every cross-curriculum team.[2] The task of devising teams of staff to work on the planning, development, implementation and evaluation of the cross-curricular themes (ie to be involved in a school development plan) will be to put into each team those members of the staff who can represent the different interests in the school.

A series of twelve questions can be put in connection with the establishment and tasks of the teams, regardless of the type of team. Each question is followed by a series of words, phrases and questions to indicate issues which will need to be addressed in response to each question.

- *What are the purposes of the teams?*

Points to consider: To plan, develop, pilot, gather and analyse data, disseminate information, discuss feedback from their own and others' work, identify and gather resources, decide time frames, decide sequences of events.

- *Who decides the team membership?*

Points to consider: Will staff self-select or be selected? Will members of the senior management decide membership? Will middle managers decide the membership?

- *Who should be in each team?*

Points to consider: Will each team contain a senior and / or middle manager? Will each team represent more than one curriculum area? Will each team have a cross-phase membership? Should teams be identical (or as near as is possible) in their membership? On what criteria will membership be decided? Will more than one teacher for each subject be included? How advantageous is it to put together departmental and / or faculty heads in one team? How advantageous is it to put together senior managers in one team?

- *What is the most appropriate size of the team?*

Points to consider: Should each team be the same size? How will overload be avoided for each team member? How will only limited participation be avoided? What is the life span of each team? Can teams be dissolved and reconstituted? How fixed, closed and permeable are the teams?

- *Will there be a team leader?*

Points to consider: Should there be a team leader? Who will be the team leader; what are her / his tasks? How will team leaders meet together to pool the findings or work of the team? Will there be a team leader or a coordinator? Will the team leader have to be a middle or senior manager? How will the appointment of team leaders be undertaken? How will disagreement and conflict be managed if a team does not have a leader?

- *What are the tasks of each team?*

Points to consider: What kinds of teams should there be (eg 'think-tank', policy forming, piloting, development, implementation, monitoring and evaluating, managerial (steering group))? Should each team undertake every type of task? Should teams replicate activities? Will one team be responsible for one theme? Will one team be responsible for many or all of the themes (if so how will this responsibility be shared within and between teams and how will this be co-ordinated? Should teams undertake different tasks? Will the planning teams be planning for themselves or for others? Will the planners be the same as the deliverers of the cross-curricular themes? What are the tasks for each team? How will the tasks be decided? How will the tasks be co-ordinated and contribute to the development and implementation of a school development plan?

- *To whom are the teams answerable?*

Points to consider: To each of its own members; to other teams; to middle managers, senior managers, governors, parents, community? For what are the teams answerable? Will different teams be answerable to the same or to different parties? Will each team be answerable to each other?

- *What are the powers of each team?*

Points to consider: Do teams have the power of veto over other teams? Is there a hierarchy of power between and within teams? On what criteria will different powers be decided and used?

- *What are the roles of each member of the team?*

Points to consider: Will different members have different roles in a team? Will roles be replicated across the teams? How will the roles be decided? Will roles change at different stages of the innovation planning and implementation? What powers are attached to each role?

- *How will teams disseminate information to each other?*

Points to consider: What form will the dissemination take − written, oral, discussion, individual or group reporting; formal, informal, a 'summary or extended report? What time scales will be in effect − how frequently and regularly will dissemination occur? Will each team be obliged to disseminate information? Who will undertake the

146

dissemination? Will each group report at the same time? How will each group's report be set into a chronological sequence? How confidential is the work of each team – what is to be made public, what will be disseminated?

- *What time frames are required in which teams will work?*
Points to consider: Will the teams be developing one theme per term or more than one theme per term? How long will the piloting take? What are the time frames for: planning and development, piloting, refinement, widespread implementation, evaluation and feedback, reformulation?

- *How will the work of the teams be monitored and evaluated?*
Points to consider: Will there be self-monitoring or monitoring by outsiders to the team? Who will set the evaluation criteria? How will results be used? Who will have access to data? How will the ethics of control and release of information be addressed? Will the same criteria be used for each group? How will the criteria change as the tasks of the group develop over time?

Three types of team

Planning and implementing the cross-curricular themes can be organized into three teams: a 'think-tank', a 'development team' and a 'piloting team'. These are discussed below.

The *think-tank* draws up the policy and plan of action in terms of tasks to be done, by whom, when and in what order. It organises the membership of the other teams and the tasks which they will perform. It is advisable to keep this team small so that it can meet easily and so that the management of discussions can be facilitated. This team has the vision and the overview and receives feedback from the development teams. Clearly it does not work in spendid isolation but will link – formally and informally – with the other teams in the school. It has the responsibility for decision making on resources, reviewing the overall development, implementation, evaluation and planning of the cross-curricular themes and initiating the next cycle of development. This team has the co-ordinating role across and through the school. It brings together the subject- or department-specific developments that have been taking place and discusses how these can be built into a whole-school framework for curriculum development and implementation. It balances the demands of different faculties and departments and ensures not only equity in distribution of resources but a curriculum for cross-curricular themes which uses timetabled time flexibly and to best effect – in line with the recommendations from the development teams. The tasks of the think tank are to ensure that final decisions on the following areas are taken:

- how the cross-curricular themes will be approached (in terms of content, organization, pedagogy);
- how the co-ordination, dissemination, discussion, development, piloting, feedback and evaluation of the proposals will take place;
- the purposes, roles, composition, tasks and time scales of development groups;
- the drawing up of the development plan – targets, tasks, initial tasks, involvement of others, the planning criteria for groups, success criteria, priorities and their representation in a chronology of events, ie to plan the management of the development.

In a primary school or small secondary school this team might include in its membership a **senior manager** who has responsibility for either curriculum development or, specifically, the development of the cross-curricular themes; one member with responsibility for **cross-phase curriculum development;** one or more **subject co-ordinators** and the teacher who has **pastoral** responsibilities. Clearly a single teacher might be fulfilling more than one of these roles, for example subject co-ordinators might have cross-phase responsibility, the teacher who has pastoral responsibility might also be a senior manager.

In a very small school the membership of this team might be the whole staff. In a large school it will include in its membership a senior manager who has responsibility for cross-curricular themes and heads of faculty to ensure that every faculty has a representative on this group, plus a member of the school who has pastoral responsibility. As with the previous example, each member of the team might be fulfilling more than one role. It is vital that an active senior member of staff is included in order that the cross-curricular themes have high status; similarly it is vital that each curriculum area by faculty representatives is included so that communication lines to all subjects are opened and used. At best this team will not be more than five or six members.

The *development team* carries out the specific curriculum planning. It makes recommendations to the think-tank about timetabling, curriculum content, resourcing, further planning, implementation and evaluation of the innovation. The development team receives feedback from the piloting teams and plans for the subsequent stage of the innovation; it provides feedback for the think-tank. It would be useful if a member of the think tank were also to be present during the meetings of the development teams. This would facilitate communication between the other teams in the school.

In a small school the development team might include a senior manager and subject co-ordinators. If one member of staff is the person designated to have responsibility for the development of the cross-curricular themes then it will be the task of this person to liaise with all of the subject co-ordinators individually and collectively during the development process so that a co-ordinated approach to development takes place. In turn the subject co-ordinators will need to take plans to, and receive feedback from, the other teachers within their field. Other teachers in the field will be involved in providing information, suggestions for planning, feedback from planning suggestions.

In a large school there will be several development teams. One development team will include the head of faculty and the subject teachers for each subject within the faculty. It may be the case that this team alone (replicated several times to cover all the subjects) will be sufficient for curriculum planning and co-ordination. However it may be the case that another development team is required which will bring together teachers from *different* departments and faculties to examine in detail the cross-curricular links which have to be made for the themes. Development teams are permeable and flexible, enabling as much information to be gathered as is required for the most workable and successful practices.

The *piloting teams,* as their name suggests, trial and pilot a small section of the innovation (however defined) and provide feedback and consequent suggestions to the development teams.

The pilot team model is less strategic, less managerially focused, less concerned with the tasks for others to undertake. It essentially fulfils a service and formative function though it can also affect the think-tank team (ie it is not solely composed of functionaries). It provides information and data on the strengths and weaknesses of one or more approaches to the implementation of the cross-curricular themes from which others might learn for their own subsequent planning. A piloting team will try out a piece of the innovation with groups of students and evaluate its effects. It is important to indicate that more than one group of students might be involved in the pilot so that attempts at representativeness of the student population might be made. The representative sampling of students is as important as the representative sampling of teachers in a pilot.

The constitution of the team will have to represent the age phases taught, the curriculum area(s) taught, a range of staff (whether within or across departments or age phases) and a range of resources. Further, there is a powerful argument to say that members of the piloting team should be drawn from the development team so that they live with their own prescriptions. The team will set its own agenda, tasks, sequences of action and time frames, submit these for consultation and refinement, provide feedback on the relative merits and demerits of particular issues and make suggestions for the improvement of practice. In this process the clarification of purposes of the pilot will then be able to be translated into operational practices.

The suggestion for a three-tier structure of planning for large institutions is an attempt to make for a workable, efficient, effective and collegial division of labour. It keeps to a minimum increased work loads for everyone. It abides by the prescriptions for successful change mentioned in the previous chapter. Clearly each team should possess a member who can communicate well within and between teams. Further, having teachers as members of more than one team facilitates communication and dissemination. Finally it enables the translation of aims and objectives in workable school development plans to be undertaken.

Exactly the same principles apply to small schools; the only difference between the small and larger school is that a three-tier system might involve the same people in all tiers, in which case the three tiers suggest *tasks* which the whole team will have to address. A compromise position here could be a two-tier system in which the tasks of the think-tank remain the same but where the tasks of the development and piloting teams are combined. Again the intention of tiering the tasks is to keep to a minimum the increased work loads that innovation usually brings.

Membership of groups should not overlook the fact that the whole staff is a group. Plenary staff meetings can be punctuated by very small 'buzz groups' which have a very specific, defined purpose and which feed back into the plenary group (cf Rodger and Richardson, 1985). Nominal group and Delphi techniques (discussed in chapter 8) can be used to expose key features, concerns, areas of consensus and priorities of issues within and between small groups or even within the whole staff.

It has been suggested that the think-tank group should develop the overall plan with due consultation with other groups and that other groups have a significant part to play in putting together the pieces of the jigsaw. This suggests that the key to success of the cross-curricular themes lies in the *divisibility* issue − divisibility of responsibilities, of tasks, of involvement, of decision making, of planning, of implementation, of evaluation. Not only is this rooted in innovation theory (eg Dalin, 1978; Fullan, 1991) but it promotes the organisational health of the school. A collegial approach recognises that any team might influence another.

The success of team approaches is not an overnight wonder. Time will have to be programmed into the school calendar for the teams to meet as frequently as is deemed necessary. Bringing together into a team those who, in the past, might not have needed to work together closely requires time for positive relationships to be developed, for ground rules of the operation of the teams to be established, and for a climate of trust and mutual dependence to be fostered.

Leadership in curriculum innovation

The argument so far has suggested that the whole project of the development of the cross-curricular themes should be the responsibility of a named senior manager. This would address the issue of accountability and give the innovation an identity which flows from having the project attached to a named person. If the named person is a senior manager then this can indicate that the innovation is important, ie it gives it status.

Allocating the overall responsibility for the innovation to a senior member of the staff can be a short-cut to linking this innovation with other innovations, resource decisions and whole-school policy development. It is often the senior management team of a school which has an overview of these other areas of the school development planning. The exercise of legitimate, earned power and authority of a senior manager can be harnessed as a force to steer the innovation and bring it to fruition. If the decision is taken not to have a senior manager with the overall responsibility for the cross-curricular themes then one can nevertheless identify some essential features of effective leadership. For example, OFSTED (1993) indicate that effective leadership should possess several characteristics:

- it is positive;
- it provides direction;
- it enables staff to understand their roles in the development of the school;
- it makes the best of people and resources available;
- it promotes positive attitudes to teaching and learning.

Morrison and Ridley (1988) expand on this by indicating that leaders require certain knowledge, skills and personality characteristics, for example:

- *knowledge* of people's motivations, what makes a school healthy, the infrastructure of the school; management styles; organizational processes; the nature of change;

- *skills* in analysing complex organisations; data collection; target setting and evaluation; managing consensus and dissensus; empathy and discretion; public relations, consultation and professional development;
- *personality characteristics* such as integrity; a reflective insight into issues; optimism and enjoyment; a willingness to take risks and to support risk taking; an ability to handle conflict and dissensus; an ability to remain calm under pressure; a tolerance of ambiguity; an ability to avoid polarizing issues, people and values; an ability to be a good listener.

It is important that the overall leader(s) (ie one person or a think-tank) should have the subject knowledge of the cross-curricular themes as well as proven expertise in curriculum development. If one of the tasks of this element of leadership is to be able to converse with the development and piloting teams then the language and focuses of those teams must be evident in the leadership.

However the notion of leadership is not confined to one individual. In the argument above one could envisage that there could be the leadership of the whole innovation which is provided by the think-tank. Moreover, within the think-tank, the development teams and the piloting teams it might be advantageous to appoint a named leader so that responsiblity is devolved and shared.

Given that there might be different leaders for different teams it is important to identify their tasks and roles. The leader of the whole innovation will have co-ordinating, communication, dissemination, consultation and legitimation functions. The leader will be answerable to the staff, governors, parents, community representatives and other relevant parties for the overall course of the innovation. The responsibility for ensuring the success of the innovation can be seen as the 'sharp end' of innovation. However, even though 'the buck' stops with this senior manager, she or he will need to affirm that collegially managed decisions bring with them shared responsibility and shared ownership. Given that innovation can meet power barriers the overall leader of the innovation will have to be prepared to be a power broker, distributing decision making appropriately amongst the participants in the innovation. At the end of the day, nevertheless, the overall leader may wish to – or have to – exercise power.

The recommendation that teamwork is the most appropriate way to plan and implement the cross-curricular themes can have its negative effects, for teams create their own territories. The commonality of purpose which makes for strong within-team bonds can also lead to

152

protectionism, factions and competition between teams. The task of the leader of the whole innovation (or the leadership team) will need to ensure that teamwork minimises the effects of these tendencies. The task will also be to maximise the importance of the several contributions to the corporate, collective innovation which are made by the participating groups. The leader has to disseminate the message that groups are different but equal, that no single group is a *primus inter pares,* and that collaboration is vital. If genuine collaboration is to occur then the mechanisms for between-group collaboration and communication must be open and utilised. The development of these mechanisms is part of the empowering role of the senior manager.

Each member of each team carries equal weight in decision making. This is a working out of democratic principles which can be used to empower individuals and groups. It also develops collegiality for successful innovation. However it might be useful administratively if each team were to have a nominal leader. The role here would be more that of spokesperson than of decision maker. This recognises the difference between power and authority. The leader of each group will have the same power as each constituent member. The group grants the team leader the authority to pass on information, recommendations, concerns and anxieties etc., to other groups and to receive feedback on these items. Each member of each team in turn will have their own measure of authority by dint of their expertise, responsibility in the school etc., Team members will have their own authority which derives from a variety of sources (cf Morrison, 1986):

- pedagogical and subject expertise;
- credibility and legitimacy in the eyes of colleagues;
- awareness of curriculum trends and developments which are taking place locally, regionally, nationally;
- understanding of interpersonal relations;
- organizational skills;
- vision;
- management skills;
- curriculum development skills and practices;
- evaluation and assesement skills;
- charisma;
- enthusiasm;
- the ability to adopt the role of the extended professional.

This set of factors recognises that leadership is multi-faceted. Without credibility and legitimacy leadership is hollow; in turn credibility and legitimacy have to be earned rather than assumed.

Summary

This chapter has argued the general case for curriculum development to be undertaken in teams and the special case for the requirement that the curriculum development of cross-curricular themes should be undertaken in teams. Teamwork was seen as a way of organising a workable and acceptable division of labour. It was suggested that the notion of leadership of the innovation and of teams was useful and necessary but that it should be democratic rather than autocratic leadership. Leadership was seen to be a function of different sources of authority. The argument suggested that recognising different sources of authority was to admit the multi-faceted nature of leadership and the fact that leadership could be a team rather than an individual property.

This chapter has argued that the management of such a large innovation as the cross-curricular themes requires a co-ordinated approach. This co-ordination, built on teamwork, enables flexibility in planning and implementation to occur. Leadership of the innovation thus has to be flexible, involving different roles, tasks and purposes. That seems to accord with the spirit of the cross-curricular themes.

Notes

1. See also Alexander (1992)
2. This is, of course, a reality for small schools.

CHAPTER EIGHT

Evaluation and the Cross-Curricular Themes

Introduction

The discussion so far has suggested that the planning, implementation and assessment of the cross-curricular themes are complex, that they go to the heart of an institution and that they affect people as well as curricula. The discussion of the cross-curricular themes as an innovation argued that people (teachers, students, managers, leaders), systems and curricula would have to change, to cover:

- aims, objectives and purposes of school;
- organisation and administration of aspects of the school;
- the organisational health and climate of the institution;
- people, behaviours, roles and relationships;
- curricula (aims, objectives, content, organisation, resourcing, teaching and learning styles, relationships with the community, assessment, planning, monitoring);
- approaches to planning;
- the management of change;
- dissemination strategies and communication channels.

If all of these factors will have to change with the planning and introduction of the cross-curricular themes then this suggests a major disturbance to existing arrangements in school. The previous chapters indicated how this could be managed through the notion of school development planning. There is clearly a necessity for ongoing evaluation of the changes and innovations if genuine improvement is to take place. The need to evaluate is underlined by OFSTED (1993) where it is made clear that evaluation and self-evaluation feature as important focuses of inspection. Further, the evaluations will be formative. Here each stage of the innovation is evaluated and the results are fed forward into subsequent planning and implementation. This chapter will suggest how the evaluation of the planning and implementation of the cross-curricular themes can operate. The touchstones here are twofold. *Firstly,* that the evaluation should be kept to a necessary minimum so that it might be practicable in a school context where any additional work could risk innovation overload and fatigue. *Secondly*, the criterion of 'fitness for purpose' should be applied, so that the evaluation will serve its formative function well.

The suggestions that the evaluations should be formative and planned follow conveniently from a view of evaluation as possessing three features:

- that *evidence* is gathered;
- that the evidence, once acquired, is *judged;*
- that the judgement leads to *decision making.*

Formative evaluation can be defined here as the collection and analysis of information so that judgements of effectiveness, worth and need can be made and that these judgements will affect decisions about the future planning and implementation of the innovation.

This chapter sets out a range of issues in planning and implementing evaluations; each institution will have to interpret these issues and tailor them to its own contexts and purposes. This chapter will not address the substance and organisation of the cross-curricular themes *per se* as the evaluation of these have already been addressed through the previous chapters. Rather it will focus on evaluating the planning and implementation of the cross-curricular themes as an example of *evaluating an innovation.* This chapter sets out a framework for evaluation which can be tailored to the specific circumstances of each school and each innovation.[1]

Approaching evaluations

It is important that evaluations should be planned. Unplanned, *ad hoc* evaluations risk lacking purpose, focus, formative potential, relevance, credibility, utility and ownership. Indeed school development plans, incorporating evaluation plans, actually require evaluation to be planned. In planning an evaluation Morrison (1993) suggests that a four-stage process can be planned, with relevant planning questions addressed at each stage:

Stage One: *Identifying the purposes of the evaluation*
Points to consider:
    (a) What purposes will the evaluation serve (eg to identify areas of strength and weakness in the planning and implementation of the

156

cross-curricular themes, to identify common and specific problems, to inform resource allocation, to identify areas to be targeted in the subsequent planning of the cross-curricular themes, to identify significant gaps between what was planned and what actually took place)?

(b) Whose purposes will the evaluation serve (eg the curriculum planners', the policy making and overall steering group's (see chapters six and seven), the leaders' of the innovation)?

Stage Two: *Identifying the priorities and constraints under which the evaluation will take place*
Points to consider:

(a) What timing and time scales are in effect?

(b) How are these timings and time scales built into a school development plan?

(c) What resources are available for the evaluation (eg human, material, temporal, financial, administrative)?

(d) Who are the audiences of the evaluation, ie which other staff or people external to the school?

(e) What are the roles and powers of the participants?

(f) How will the evaluation be reported and used, ie how will its formative function actually occur?

Stage Three: *Planning the evaluation within identified constraints*
Points to consider:

(a) What questions will the evaluation ask and answer (and how will these be generated − see the discussion in chapters six and seven of the planning of the management of the cross-curriular themes)?

(b) Upon what will the evaluation focus (in terms of the eight major areas outlined in the introduction to this chapter − (i) aims and purposes of the school, (ii) organization and administration, (iii) organizational health and climate, (iv) people and curricula, (v) approaches to planning, (vi) management of change, (vii) dissemination strategies, (viii) communication channels)?

(c) Who owns the evaluation data (eg those who yield it, those to whom it is yielded, those who subsequently receive the evaluation)?

(d) Will the evaluation gather numerical and / or word-based data − how will these different approaches serve the purposes of the evaluation (for example numerical data might indicate frequencies and strengths of feeling about an issue, word-based data might enable candid, extended and highlighted − prioritised − feedback to be gathered)?

157

(e) What methods of gathering information are most suitable (eg *written* and *non-written* forms?
(f) Which people will be most suitable to go to for the information and how representative will they need to be of a wider school staff?
(g) How will reliability and validity be addressed?
(h) How will information be processed and reported (and to whom)?
(i) How will the results of the ongoing evaluations be built into the subsequent planning and development of the innovation?

Stage Four: *Agreeing the operation of the evaluation*
Points to consider:
(a) How will agreement on the questions set out above be addressed?
(b) How will disagreement be managed?
(c) Who will carry out the evaluation, ie which members of staff will be involved for different areas of the evaluation – curriculum planners, leaders of the innovation, senior and middle managers, steering groups and co-ordinating bodies in the school, policy makers, heads of departments, heads of faculty, heads of subjects / teachers with responsibility for subjects, heads of age groups)?
(d) Will there be one evaluating group or several (eg will teachers and planners in one area of the innovation evaluate their own plans, implementation and outcomes and report to a co-ordinating group, or will one group undertake all of the evaluation throughout the school – keeping an overview and feeding back the evaluation information to different groups – the planners, policy makers, co-ordinators, steering groups, whole staff, curriculum development groups)?
(e) Will colleagues be evaluating themselves or will colleagues be evaluated by others in the school?

This list of points appears to be lengthy. However it does ensure:

(i)   that evaluations will be as formal or informal as required;
(ii) that the procedures for bringing the evaluations into a formative development plan are assured and made explicit (the issue of *clarity,* a fundamental concern in innovations);
(iii) that the 'rules of the game' are negotiated before the project is undertaken rather than the rules being altered or made up as the project proceeds.

It can be seen, then, that just as in a school development plan, the planning of an evaluation might take nearly as long as the implementation. If a formative evaluation is to be effective then the

158

planning of that evaluation itself is part of the planning of the innovation.

This series of points can apply to large schools, to medium sized schools and to small schools; the only difference between their application will be in their management. For example a large school might need to plan an infrastructure or network of discussions and discussion groups to negotiate and agree the planning and operation of the formative evaluations whereas in a smaller school this can be managed with the whole staff together.

Gathering evaluation data

There is a battery of data collection instruments available to the evaluator covering *written forms* and *live, interpersonal* forms. These can be set out as seen in Figure 8.1.

Figure 8.1 – Instruments for Data Collection

WRITTEN FORMS OF DATA COLLECTION
Delphi techniques; diaries; journals; logs; questionnaires using closed response formats; questionnaires using open-ended response formats; documents (eg reports, records, minutes); survey data; test results; content analysis; resource analysis; sociometry
LIVE, INTERPERSONAL FORMS OF DATA COLLECTION
Nominal group technique; evaluation meetings; interviews (structured, semi-structured, unstructured); observation (structured, semi-structured, unstructured); snowball techniques

This does not exhaust the ways of acquiring evaluation information. However, given the pressures on staff it is unrealistic to expect vast amounts of evaluation data to be gathered by a vast selection of instruments. In order to avoid work overload it is suggested that evaluations will draw on the following main methods of acquiring data:

- nominal group techniques (discussed below);
- Delphi techniques (discussed below);
- published evaluation instruments (discussed below);
- minutes of meetings (eg discussions), either kept as minutes or transcribed into a brief report;
- targeted interviews (ie interviews where a clear agenda has been set) – individual or group (minuted or written up in another form during or after the interview);
- informal discussions which are then put into formal interim reports.

Whilst the contents of these six methods will be a matter for discussion the following sections provide guidelines on what these might be.

It was suggested in chapter seven that a team approach to planning, implementing and evaluating the cross-curricular themes might be useful. Each team could devise its own instruments for data collection (formal and informal) or use published instruments. A very rapid method of information acquisition is the nominal group technique and its partner, the Delphi technique (Morrison, 1993). In the nominal group technique participants are asked to write down – with no discussion with others – their responses to questions or statements put by the evaluator(s). These are then written onto a large sheet of paper for others to view. The evaluator asks for individual comments on the items displayed, again without discussion; the comments are written by the relevant item on the large sheet. The evaluator then asks participants to identify clusters of issues, ie to start to introduce structures and highlights into the items displayed. This is done by the group in an open discussion, the outcome of which is an identification of key issues put into a priority order and thus collectively 'owned' by the group, incorporating an individual's response within a group response.

With a large group there might be a tiering of data collection using a *snowball* technique wherein an individual response is shared with a partner, then that group of two shares responses with another group of two and so on until the whole group has come together. If a snowball technique is to be used then a spokesperson will have to be appointed for each group at each stage of reporting. The nominal group and snowball techniques are useful ways of addressing team responses, collegiality and focused outcomes of discussions.

A variant of this approach is the Delphi technique wherein the evaluator asks participants to write down responses to questions or statements, either individually or in groups (eg teams, departments, subject groups, age phases). She then collects these responses and collates them into clusters of issues and responses. These are passed back to groups (either with the same or reconstituted membership) for subsequent comment and discussion in order to identify priorities and key issues, ie a group response is sought. This process is repeated as many times as thought fit until general agreement is reached by the whole staff or large group. What is taking place in this process is an identification of key issues and a polarising of response — areas of general agreement and areas of disagreement. In addition to identifying significant areas of an issue the attraction of this approach is that, because the responses are presented in writing and collated and re-written by the evaluator, the individual's responses are anonymous, enabling honesty to be addressed. Further, because the responses are written down, it might not be necessary for groups or a whole staff to meet together, a major factor for busy staff. However it does place a lot of work onto the shoulders of the evaluator who has to collate, summarise and pass back data back to participants in several cycles.

Both of these techniques accord equal voice to all participants, which is useful in promoting collegiality and the practice of democracy in institutions. They build in involvement and lead to a clarification of issues and priorities, both of which are significant determinants of successful innovation. In a situation in education where time is a precious commodity these two techniques are valuable time-saving devices for gathering and using information.

Examples of *published* instruments which teams could use are:

(i) the *DION Handbook: Diagnosis of Individual and Organisational Needs for Staff Development and In-Service Training in Schools* (Elliott-Kemp and Williams, 1979) which can be used quickly to assess the organisational health of an institution and its specific areas of strength and weakness;

(ii) specific short tasks which can be undertaken in staff development sessions (Rodger and Richardson, 1985, ch. 3);

(iii) the *Concerns Questionnaire* (Hall *et al*, 1979) which can be used quickly to identify the concerns which participants have about an innovation. These are sufficiently focused to be valuable for addressing the concerns and responsibilities of the team, particularly the 'think-tank' team (discussed below).

Additionally OFSTED (1993) provide a high level of detail of inspections which schools can easily turn into evaluation instruments.

Implementing the evaluation

Different participants will play different roles in formative evaluation. This can be devolved on the three-team approach advocated in the last chapter: the *think-tank* team which is concerned with policy, overall co-ordination and steering; the *development* team which is concerned with the practicalities of planning and implementation; the *piloting* team which is concerned with trialling aspects of the innovation with a selection of staff and students.

Each team will be both *instigating* and *receiving* evaluations and evaluation data, though the piloting team will tend to undertake rather that to instigate evaluations. If teachers are members of more than one team then communication of evaluation findings can be facilitated. There will be common concerns which straddle the three teams:

- making judgements of *effectiveness and worthwhileness;*
- making judgements of the *efficacy* of team approaches to planning and implementation;
- the identification of *strengths, weaknesses and problematical areas;*
- *the identification of positive and negative* aspects of areas of the innovation;
- the identification of the nature and degree of cross-curricularity;
- an indication of particular *concerns* in the planning and implementation of the themes;
- the identification of factors which are *facilitating* and *inhibiting* the development of the themes;
- the identification of areas of *agreement* and *disagreement* in planning and implementation of the cross-curricular themes;
- the nature and extent of the *impact* of the planning and implementation on participants (including teachers, students, participants from the community);
- the areas of *improvement* and areas of *poor progress* in students who have been involved in the implementation of the cross-curricular themes;
- the *strength of feeling* amongst the participants about factors in the development and implementation of the cross-curricular themes;

- the making of *recommendations* for the further effectiveness and / or modification of the innovation, eg in terms of resources, roles, staffing, in-service development, planning styles, scope of change etc., ie making recommendations in the light of the evaluations undertaken.

It is possible to identify the evaluation tasks for each team thus:

(i) Evaluation tasks of the think-tank team:

With regard to *instigating* evaluations it will need to assess:

- the organisational health of the school;
- the concerns and anxieties of staff;
- the ways in which the aims and objectives of the innovation impact on the aims and objectives of the school and *vice-versa;*
- the organisational and administrative implications for the school of the implementation of the cross-curricular themes;
- the decisions which teams will have to and have taken in planning and implementing the cross-curricular themes;
- the implications for, and effects of, the development and implementation of the cross-curricular themes on *people, behaviours, roles* and *relationships, teams* (tasks and membership);
- *curricula* – in summary form – (to include aims, objectives, content, organisation, resourcing, teaching and learning styles, relationships with the community, assessment, planning, monitoring), *dissemination.*

This team will require only sufficient data so that an overview of policy, co-ordination and developments can be monitored.

The tasks of this team will also be built into the school development plans in terms of objectives, routes to the achievement of these objectives and criteria for judging the success of these objectives. This is clearly an objectives model of evaluation. Though it might not allow for unexpected outcomes this sets the criteria for evaluation very clearly — the extent to which the objectives for the teams have been achieved — and the identification of facilitating and inhibiting factors which have had a bearing on the outcomes.

With regard to *receiving* evaluation information from other groups the think-tank will require summary evaluation information on the developments and trialling of the planned innovations from the other two groups. This can be done in a written or an oral report, by individuals from other teams or in a group, by individuals in the think-tank or by the whole of the think-tank togther. The information required will be similar to that of the *instigated* evaluations in outline but it will differ in one important respect. Whereas the *instigated* evaluation was concerned with overarching, general factors the *received* information will seek to identify how these factors are working out in practice with reference to specific departments, subject areas, phases etc. Though this information will be in summary form it will be addressing issues concerned with the practical planning and implementation of the cross-curricular themes, ie how these are impacting on the other teams and teachers involved. This will enable the think-tank team to look for common issues, concerns, practices, development and to compare one development team's practices with another, ie to gather information which can feed into a co-ordinated approach. What has been suggested is that the think-tank will require more formal reporting than takes place in the other two teams.

This team does not work in isolation from others, simply receiving summaries and handing down prescriptions for development. Rather it is involved in discussions and dissemination in ways outlined in chapter seven. It has a complementary rather than autocratic and directive role to play in the development and implementation of the cross-curricular themes.

(ii) Evaluation tasks of the development team

The development team builds the curriculum for the cross-curricular themes. Therefore it will address specific planning and development issues. These might include: curriculum statements, teachers' and students' tasks, teachers' concerns, teachers' and students' knowledge, curriculum organisation and structure, approaches to delivery, resourcing, styles of teaching and learning, assessment, record-keeping, sharing of development issues, of information.

In *instigating* evaluations it will use the items indicated in the previous chapters as criteria to evaluate the *effectiveness* of the planning and implementation of the themes. It will identify *particular issues, problems, strengths, weaknesses* in developing the themes, the *results of piloting* the developments and the *extent* to which the development team has been able to address significant identified issues. These will cover, for example:

- the coverage of the content of the themes (expressed in terms of objectives, knowledge, skills, attitudes, key concepts, range of teaching styles etc.) discussed in chapters two and three and related to those criteria (eg flexibility, avoidance of overlap, progression and continuity, use of the environment etc.);

- the management of an innovation which is characterised by its large scale, complexity, systemic nature, eg to evaluate its clarity, divisibility, communicability, triallability, consonance with existing practices, acceptability to the values of teachers and the school ethos, organisational structures, practicability, discussed in chapter six;
- the ways in which timetabling arrangements have been addressed (eg the issues raised in chapter four concerning flexibility and the use of a variety of different timetabling arrangements) and reduction of timetable overload;
- the ways in which the curriculum involves community groups, the development of relationships with the community, the use of the community resources (discussed in chapters two–five);
- the planning approaches adopted (discussed in chapter three);
- the development, co-ordination and implementation of assessment and record keeping (discussed in chapter five);
- the decisions which the development team has had to take in planning and implementing the innovation;
- the involvement of team members in addressing the following:
    additional tasks required of them and additions to workloads;
    their abilities to change roles and relationships, teaching and learning styles;
    their involvement in deskilling and reskilling;
    liaising with colleagues and outside agencies with whom they have had limited prior contact;
    developing collaborative planning and co-ordinated teaching;
    making contributions to school development plans;
    taking seriously the concerns and anxieties of participants;
- the provision of adequate resources for planning — material, in-service, human, financial, administrative, temporal — discussed in chapter six;
- the costs and benefits of the innovation — human, material, temporal — discussed in chapter six;
- the issues of staff morale, identification of anxieties and concerns, and the raising and lowering of anxieties and concerns (discussed in chapters six and seven);
- the identification of unexpected outcomes;
- the dissemination of the innovation and its several aspects (discussed in chapters six and seven).

As with the think-tank team the operations of the development team will be incorporated into the school development plan, ie this team will have set its objectives, routes to the achievement of these objectives and success criteria for its work. These can become part of the evaluation. Additionally, because the development team will be identifying the objectives of the curriculum the achievement of these curricular objectives will also become a part of the evaluation. This will require identification of successes, problems, issues arising in practice, factors which are determining success or its lack.

The instigation of evaluations by the development team will not be confined to its own work, ie self-evaluation, for this team sets the tasks for the piloting teams (in collaboration with the members of those teams). For example, it will provide the agenda for the piloting team in terms of indicating to the piloting team the purposes of the pilot and the areas in which to work. It is a matter for negotiation whether the pilot team will be given latitude to interpret these in ways which they think appropriate or whether the development team will be highly specific and prescriptive, with the pilot team implementing these requirements to the letter. The development team themselves might be affected by feedback from other development teams or might be part of a cross-development-team uniform strategy undertaken so that comparisons between teams can be made.

This team will *receive* evaluation information from the other two teams. From the think-tank team it will receive feedback about the overall development and comparable development in which other teams have been involved. From the piloting teams it will receive feedback on the trialling of specific pieces of the innovation. Hence the development team also has a co-ordinating function in planning, receiving and acting on evaluations. The evaluations for which the development team will be responsible will be less formal that those required by the think-tank although, clearly, some formal data acquisition and reporting will have to occur.

(iii) Evaluation tasks of the piloting team

The piloting team has a much tighter remit than the other two teams; though it can both *undertake* and *receive* evaluations the likelihood of its actually *instigating* evaluations is limited as this team is a functionary of the development team. The piloting team will be involved in:

- trialling materials and curricula with groups of students and reporting on their strengths and weaknesses;

166

- identifying areas which need further development;
- identifying the effectiveness, strengths, weaknesses and problematical issues in resourcing, organisation, effectiveness of teaching and learning styles; the extent to which the objectives of the piece of the curriculum have been achieved and the worthwhileness of the objectives; specific factors which have facilitated or inhibited success;
- making recommendations for improvements to the programmes.

Here an evaluation will chart the consonance between what was intended to be the case and what actually turned out to be the case (Stake, 1976). This can be undertaken in terms of:

- Intended and actual contexts, initial states and starting points *(antecedents)*.

For example, this would indicate whether the plans were suitably cognizant of the reality of classrooms; students (existing knowledge, prior curricula, prior experiences, abilities); teachers; resources; curricula.

- Intended and actual practices *in situ (transactions)*.

For example, this would include introductions; teaching and learning styles; ways of organising lessons and students; balancing student and teacher freedom and autonomy with direction and control; discipline and the management of acceptable behaviour; accessing and using resources; assessment and testing; sequencing lessons; organising time.

- Intended and actual products and effects *(outcomes)*.

For example, this would include reactions of teachers and students to the programme, motivational potential, student behaviours, achievements and performances, comparative successes and failures.

All of these points feature highly as inspection focuses by OFSTED (1993). As mentioned earlier the degree of autonomy of the pilot team might be negotiable. At one extreme the pilot team will be implementing to the letter the fine detail provided by the development team of what to undertake, how, when and in what order to undertake it, how to assess, evaluate and record it. At the other extreme the pilot team will have a greater degree of autonomy in trialling materials and curricula with the result that each pilot is more like one or more case studies. It is the piloting team which provides the raw data for the development team. In a formative evaluation, where data from a pilot feed into subsequent planning, there need to be plentiful formal and informal channels of communication. This will enable results to be built into developments quickly and to ensure that the pilot team is fully apprised of the nature and purposes of the pilot. Pilot teams are the 'ground troops' (if the metaphor is appropriate!); the success of an exercise depends upon rapid intelligence between all the teams involved. As with the development team, it is likely that the piloting team will undertake fewer formal evaluations than the think-tank (constraints of time may be a significant factor in deciding this).

Summary

This chapter has addressed the contents, purposes, criteria, formality and informality, management and tasks of evaluating the planning and implementation of the cross-curricular themes as innovations. The need for evaluation was seen to be not only *per se* but to serve inspection purposes very clearly. Because the introduction of the cross-curricular themes represents a complex and systemic innovation it was suggested that an evaluation of this innovation would have a wide field of focus and content. It was argued that for evaluations to be economical on time and to be purposeful they need to be planned and to be fitted into school development plans.

Further, because formative evaluations serve many purposes the argument suggested that the nature, focus and methodology of evaluations should be mindful of 'fitness for purpose'. Combining the notion of 'fitness for purpose' with the need to address economies of time suggested that even though a wide range of data collection techniques is available the reality of the situation is that only a limited range of data collection instruments might be useful. These were outlined and suggestions made for how they could be used.

Building on the argument in chapter seven that a team approach to planning would save time through a division of labour this chapter has argued that the same could apply to evaluation activity. The nature of different approaches to and content of evaluation within a team approach were discussed. The balance of formal and informal evaluations was seen to be a function of the purposes of the teams. It was argued that though some formal reporting was useful for feedback and feedforwards for all participants it was likely to be the case that the think-tank team would be using more formal evaluations and evaluation reports. Indeed the case was made for formality to be minimised and informality to be developed, particularly for the development and piloting teams.[2] Though different teams would have different evaluation tasks the chapter demonstrated that there was a commonality of evaluation criteria, purposes, focuses and methods and indicated what these were.

The main feature of an evaluation is that it should be useful. This is particularly the case in formative evaluations where subsequent decisions are based on information received. One of the messages of this book has been that the development of cross-curricular themes is premised on collegiality. This chapter has argued that decision making is the province of all sectors of the school; it has also demonstrated how collegial evaluations can be undertaken and how they can feed into collegial decision making.

Notes

1. Morrison (1993) sets out a comprehensive guide to school-centred evaluation which can be used across phases and which balances utility with fine detail.

2. The need for documentation to be made available for school inspections might require formal records and reports to be kept.

Postscript

The planning and implementation of the cross-curricular themes is a marvellous opportunity for staff to engage in forms of working with each other which they may not have encountered before. All too frequently individuals, subjects teams and age phase teams work in isolation from each other. This can be a major obstacle to effective innovation (Hargreaves, 1989). The recent literature on school effectiveness (eg Mortimore *et al,* 1988; Galvin *et al,* 1990; Alexander, 1992; Alexander, Rose and Woodhead, 1992) speaks in unison of the value of a whole-school approach to planning and implementing policy. Consistency of practice promotes a positive school environment. This book has suggested that consistency tempered with flexibility is an unavoidable ingredient in planning the cross-curricular themes. It has indicated how this might be approached.

Not only do the cross-curricular themes present school staff with opportunities to work together in new ways but it has been demonstrated in this book that the cross-curricular themes enable out-of-school colleagues in the community to play an important part in education. The school reaches into the community and the community reaches into the school. The dialogue between all the stakeholders in education – students, teachers, parents, governors, community representatives etc – has a common focus in the cross-curricular themes. This can operate to the advantage of all parties.

The school curriculum is currently (and constantly) in flux; teachers have to live with change just as students will have to live with change beyond school. In a climate of change and rapid innovation the need for mutual support comes to the fore. It has been argued that the development of the cross-curricular themes enables a climate of support to be fostered within and beyond the school whilst updating of the curriculum takes place.

The cross-curricular themes require active and experiential learning; that recognises that most students have active, enquiring minds and that

170

this can be harnessed to work on central issues for the twenty-first century – the ability to be an active citizen of a variety of communities, cultures and societies. The content and process (pedagogy) of the cross-curricular themes are mutually supporting and are firmly rooted in the social basis of learning (a central feature in effective learning). It appears, then, that this aspect of the whole curriculum is a focus for significant issues in education: its relationship to society, its development of the individual, its development of creativity, its opportunity for enjoyable and valuable learning and its preparation of future adults.

In this respect the five cross-curricular themes addressed in this book are a subset of a whole variety of new additional cross-curricular initiatives that are taking place in schools. These cover, for example: curriculum *content* (eg education about Europe, enterprise education), *pedagogy* (eg problem-solving strategies, flexible and collaborative learning, action planning and negotiated learning), *skills* (eg information technology, personal and social skills), *attitudes* (eg caring for the environment, tolerance of diversity) and *issues* (eg equal opportunities, multicultural and gender awareness, special educational needs). This book has not attempted to deal with all of these. Instead it has taken the agenda of the national curriculum cross-curricular themes and shown how these can impact of everyday school practice. The literature on cross-curricular matters is expanding. However this book deliberately has gone to 'first principles' in looking at the five *Curriculum Guidance* documents from the National Curriculum Council. This was done in the interests of clarity, in order that readers could train their eyes on issues of planning and implementation rather than on detailed matters of curriculum content. The case was made for regarding a major element of the success of the cross-curricular themes as being their manageability. This book has striven to render manageable the complexity of what is one of the most significant innovations in education. Manageability is a key to the success of an innovation.

It has been suggested through this book that the cross-curricular themes can be a major force for empowerment. They bring together people and communities. In indicating how this might be realized in practice it has been argued here that empowerment, like freedom, requires more than acceptance; it needs understanding and critique to work in tandem for democracy. The cross-curricular themes have a major contribution to make to the freedoms, creativity and development of individuals, groups, communities and society. As Jacob Bronowski once remarked: 'we must touch people'.

Bibliography

Alexander R. (1992) *Policy and Practice in Primary Education.* London: Routledge.
Alexander R., Rose J. and Woodhead C. (1992) *Curriculum Organization and Classroom Practice in Primary Schools: a Discussion Paper.* London: HMSO.
Apple M. (1990) *Ideology and Curriculum* (second edition). London: Routledge.
Apple M. (1993a) *Official Knowledge: Democratic Education in a Conservative Age.* New York: Routledge.
Apple M. (1993b) 'The politics of official knowledge: does a national curriculum makes sense?' *Teachers College Record,* 95 (2), pp. 222–241.
Bernstein B. (1971) 'On the classification and framing of educational knowledge,' in M. F. D. Young (ed.) *Knowledge and Control.* Basingstoke: Collier-Macmillan.
Bourdieu P. (1976) 'The school as a conservative force', in R. Dale *et al* (eds.) *Schooling and Capitalism.* London: Routledge and Kegan Paul.
Bowring-Carr C. (1993) 'How shall we know quality in teaching and learning? Some problems associated with classroom observation', *The Curriculum Journal,* 4 (3), pp. 315–333.
Bruner J. (1960) *The Process of Education.* New York: Random House.
Buck M. and Inman S. (1992) *Whole School Provision for Personal and Social Development: The Role of the Cross Curricular Elements* (Curriculum Guidance No 1), London, Centre for Cross Curricular Initiatives, Goldsmiths' College, University of London.
Central Advisory Council for Education (CACE) *Children and Their Primary Schools* (Plowden Report). London: HMSO.
Cresswell M. J. and Houghton J. G. (1991 'Assessment of the National Curriculum: some fundamental considerations'. *Educational Review,* 43 (1), pp. 63–78.
Cuban L. (1990) 'A fundamental puzzle of school reform', in A. Lieberman (ed.) *Schools as Collaborative Cultures.* Lewes: Falmer.
Dalin P. (1978) *Limits to Educational Change.* London: Macmillan.
Dalin P. and Rust V. D. (1983) *Can Schools Learn?* Windsor: NFER-Nelson.
Dalin P., Rolff H. G. and Kleekamp B. (1993) *Changing the School Culture.* London: Cassell.
Davis E. (1983) *Teachers as Curriculum Evaluators.* London: Allen and Unwin.
Department for Education (1993) *The Education Reform Act 1988: The Education (National Curriculum) (Assessment Arrangements for the Core Subjects) (Key Stage 1) Order 1993,* (Circular 11/93). London: DFE.
Department of Education and Science (1985) *The Curriculum from 5–16.* London: HMSO.
Department of Education and Science (1987) *The National Curriculum 5–16: a Consultation Document.* London: HMSO.

172

Department of Education and Science (1988a) *The Education Reform Act 1988: The School Curriculum and Assessment.* London: HMSO.

Department of Education and Science (1988b *National Curriculum Task Group on Assessment and Testing: a Report.* London: HMSO.

Department of Education and Science (1989) *Planning for School Development.* London: HMSO.

Department of Education and Science (1990) *Technology in the National Curriculum.* London: HMSO.

Department of Education and Science (1991a) *Geography in the National Curriculum (England).* London: HMSO.

Department of Education and Science (1991b) *Science in the National Curriculum.* London: HMSO.

Department of Education and Science (1991c) *Mathematics in the National Curriculum.* London: HMSO.

Department of Education and Science (1992) *Physical Education in the National Curriculum.* London: HMSO.

Dewey J. (1954) *The Public and Its Problems.* Ohio: Swallow Press.

Dixon R. (1977) *Catching Them Young (1): Sex, Race and Class in Children's Fiction.* London: Pluto Press.

Elliott-Kemp J., and Williams, G. L. (1979) *The DION Handbook: Diagnosis of Individual and Organisational Needs for Staff Development and In-Service Training in Schools.* Sheffield: Sheffield City Polytechnic.

Eraut M. *et al* (1991) *Flexible Learning in Schools.* Sheffield: Training Agency.

Fullan M. (1991) *The New Meaning of Educational Change.* London: Cassell.

Galvin P., Mercia S. and Costa P. (1990) *Building a Better Behaved School.* Harlow: Longman.

Giroux H. (1983) *Theory and Resistance in Education.* London: Heinemann.

Grundy S. (1987) *Curriculum: Product or Praxis.* Lewes: Falmer.

Habermas J. (1972) *Knowledge and Human Interests* (trans. J. Shapiro). London: Heinemann.

Hall G. E., George A. and Rutherford W. L. (1979) *Measuring Stages of Concern about the Innovation: a Manual for Use of the SOC Questionnaire.* Austin: University of Austin at Texas.

Hall G. and Hord S. (1987) *Change in Schools.* New York: State University of New York Press.

Halsey A. H. (1992) 'An international comparison of access to higher education', in D. Phillips (ed.) *Lessons of Cross-national Comparison in Education.* Wallingford: Triangle Books.

Hargreaves A. (1989) *Curriculum and Assessment Reform.* Oxford: Basil Blackwell and the Open University Press.

Hargreaves D. G. (1991) 'Coherence and manageability: reflections on the National Curriculum and cross-curricular provision', *The Curriculum Journal,* 2 (1) 1991, pp. 33–42.

Hargreaves D. H. and Hopkins D. (1991) *The Empowered School.* London: Cassell.

Harwood D. (1985) 'We need political not Political Education for 5-13 year olds', *Education 3-13,* 13 (1), pp. 12–17.

Havelock R. (1973) *The Change Agent's Guide to Innovation in Education.* New Jersey: Englewood Cliffs.

Hirst P. (1975) 'The curriculum and its objectives – a defence of piecemeal rational planning', *The Doris Lee Lectures.* London: University of London Press.

Hohmann M., Bunet B. and Weikart D. W. (1979) *Young Children in Action.* Michigan: The High Scope Press.

Hoy W. K., Tarter C. J. and Kottkamp R. B. (1991) *Open Schools, Healthy Schools.* London: Sage Publications Ltd.

Hoyle E. (1975) 'The creativity of the school in Britain', in A. Harris *et al* (eds.) *Curriculum Innovation.* London: Croom Helm and the Open University Press.

Huberman M. and Miles M. (1984) *Qualitative Data Analysis.* Beverly Hills: Sage Publications.

Hughes J. A. (1976) *Sociological Analysis: Methods of Discovery.* Middlesex: Thomas Nelson and Sons Ltd.

Inner London Education Authority (ILEA) (1989) *The Primary Language Record: Handbook for Teachers.* London: Inner London Education Authority.

Jausovec N. (1990) 'Education in Yugoslavia-Slovenia', *The Curriculum Journal,* 1 (3), pp. 255–263.

Kerr J. F. (1968) *Changing the Curriculum.* London: University of London Press.

Knight B. (1991) *Designing the School Day: a Do-it yourself Manual.* Harlow: Longman.

Law B. (1984) *Uses and Abuses of Profiling.* London: Harper and Row.

Lieberman A. (ed.) (1991) *Schools as Collaborative Cultures.* Lewes: Falmer.

Lowes B. (1992) 'Case study', in K. R. B. Morrison, *Curriculum Planning for Cross-curricular Issues,* course documentation for the Masters degree in Education, School of Education, University of Durham.

McGuiness J. B. (1989) *A Whole School Approach to Pastoral Care.* London: Kogan Page.

McKenzie C. (1990) 'Cross-curricular dissensions', *Education,* 176 (18, p. 374.

Miles M. (1975) Planned change and organisational health, in A. Harris *et al* (eds.) *Curriculum Innovation.* London: Croom Helm and the Open University Press.

Moon B. (1988) *Modular Curriculum.* London: Paul Chapman Publishing.

Morrison K. R. B. (1986) 'Primary school subject specialists as agents of school-based curriculum change', *School Organization,* 6 (2) pp. 175–183.

Morrison K. R. B. (1989) 'Bringing progressivism into a critical theory of education'. *British Journal of Sociology of Education,* 10 (1), pp. 3–18.

Morrison K. R. B. (1992) *Curriculum Planning for Cross-curricular Issues,* course documentation for the Masters degree in Education, School of Education, University of Durham.

Morrison K. R. B. (1993) *Planning and Accomplishing School-Centred Evaluation.* Norfolk: Peter Francis Publishers.

Morrison K. R. B. and Ridley K. (1988) *Curriculum Planning and the Primary School.* London: Paul Chapman Publishing.

Mortimore P. *et al* (1988), *School Matters: the Junior Years.* Shepton Mallet: Open Books.

National Curriculum Council (1989a) *A Framework for the Primary Curriculum.* York: National Curriculum Council.

National Curriculum Council (1989b) *A Curriculum for All.* York: National Curriculum Council.

National Curriculum Council (1990a) *The Whole Curriculum.* York: National Curriculum Council.

National Curriculum Council (1990b) *Education for Economic and Industrial Understanding.* York: National Curriculum Council.

National Curriculum Council (1990c) *Health Education.* York: National Curriculum Council

National Curriculum Council (1990d) *Careers Education and Guidance.* York: National Curriculum Council.

National Curriculum Council (1990e) *Environmental Education.* York: National Curriculum Council.

National Curriculum Council (1990f) *Education for Citizenship.* York: National Curriculum Council.

Nuttall D. (1988) 'The implications of national curriculum assessments', *Educational Psychology,* 8 (4), pp. 221–229).

Office for Standards in Education (OFSTED) (1993) *Handbook for the Inspection of Schools.* London: OFSTED.

Read H. (1958) *Education Through Art.* London: Faber.

Rodger I. and Richardson J. A. S. (1985) *Self-Evaluation for Primary Schools.* Sevenoaks: Hodder and Stoughton.

Rutter M. *et al* (1979) *Fifteen Thousand Hours.* Shepton Mallet: Open Books.

Ryan A. (1992) Case study, in K. R. B. Morrison, *op cit.*

Schools Council (1981) *The Practical Curriculum,* working paper 70. London: Methuen.

Schools Curriculum and Assessment Authority (SCAA) (1993a) *Final Report: The National Curriculum and Its Assessment (Ron Dearing.* London: SCAA.

Schools Curriculum and Assessment Authority (SCAA) (1993b) *School Curriculum Folder, Information and Guidance about Assessment Arrangements in 1994.* London: SCAA.

Skilbeck M. (1984) *School-Based Curriculum Development.* London: Harper and Row.

Smyth J. (1989) 'A critical pedagogy of classroom practice', *Journal of Curriculum Studies,* 21 (6), pp. 483–502.

Smyth J. (1991) *Teachers as Collaborative Learners.* Milton Keynes: Open University Press.

Stenhouse L. (1975) *An Introduction to Curriculum Research and Development.* London: Heinemann.

Taba H. (1962) *Curriculum Development: Theory and Practice.* New York: Harcourt, Brace and World.

Tyler R. W. (1949) *Basic Principles of Curriculum and Instruction.* Chicago: University of Chicago Press.

Wheeler D. K. (1967) *Basic Curriculum Process.* London: University of London Press.

Whetton C., Ruddock G. and Hopkins S. (1991), *The Pilot Study of Standard Assessment Tasks for Key Stage 1: A Report.* London: Schools Examinations and Assessment Council.

Wilcox B. (1992) *Time-Constrained Evaluation.* London: Routledge.

Wiliam D. (1993) 'Validity, dependability and reliability in National Curriculum assessment', *The Curriculum Journal,* 4 (3), pp. 335–350.

Worsley P. (1977) *Introducing Sociology* (second edition). Harmondsworth: Penguin.

Young M. F. D. (1971) 'An approach to the study of curricula as socially organized knowledge', in M. F. D. Young (ed.) *Knowledge and Control.* Basingstoke: Collier-Macmillan.

Index

Note: where several references are given, the bold numbers indicate the most important page numbers